Utopia

To live now, as human beings should live,
in defiance of all that is bad around us, is
itself a marvellous victory.

Howard Zinn

Utopia

Five Leaves Publications
www.fiveleaves.co.uk

Utopia
Edited by Ross Bradshaw

Published by Five Leaves Publications,
PO Box 8786, Nottingham NG1 9AW
www.fiveleaves.co.uk
ISBN: 978-907869-50-1

Five Leaves acknowledges
financial support from
Arts Council England

Five Leaves is represented
to the book trade by Turnaround
and distributed by Central Books

Original cover design for series
Richard Hollis

Typeset and designed by
Four Sheets Design and Print

Contents

Introduction

A year ago Five Leaves brought out the first of its annual collections of essays, *Maps*. We were conscious that one country not mentioned was the one we most wish to visit, Utopia. This collection of essays is much bigger than we intended as there is so much to say about real and fictional utopian living. We are aware that we have still only scratched the surface.

If any justification is needed for a compendium on this subject, other than having a healthy interest in William Morris, read the opening essay by Mike Marqusee (one of no doubt many American Jewish Marxist cricket-lovers) suggesting that those who want *any* kind of progressive society must hold to a vision of a better future, a utopia, as well as campaigning against war, poverty and disease in the present. Read his essay then turn to the old poster from the *Country Standard* at the back of the book. The writers of that journal – recently relaunched – hated rural poverty, the terrible wages and conditions for agricultural workers, the tied-cottage system, the squirearchy, but kept a vision in mind of what a different countryside could be like.

This compendium, like the others in the series, is a mixture of material "from the vaults", from work in progress and material specially written for the collection. The writers are a mixture of regular and irregular contributors to Five Leaves' books and others close to the press but who usually publish elsewhere, supplemented by writers from the past including William Morris and Marie Louise Berneri.

Utopia is dedicated to the late Peter Preston, the author of the longest essay in the book. Peter was a long-time activist in the William Morris Society and a great friend of

Five Leaves. He died ten months ago. The overwhelming turnout at his memorial meeting was a tribute to his work with the Morris Society, his long career in adult education and in keeping alive interest in D.H. Lawrence. Peter shared Five Leaves' interests in London fiction, secular Jewish culture, Nottingham and, of course, utopia.

Ross Bradshaw
Five Leaves
September 2012

Let's Talk Utopia

Mike Marqusee

In 1818, Shelley visited his friend Byron in Venice, where his Lordship was camped out in a decaying *palazzo*, ruminating on the city's faded glories. Their conversations — on human freedom and the prospects for social change — formed the basis for Shelley's poem *Julian and Maddalo*, in which the mild-mannered English rationalist Julian (Shelley) puts the case for hope while the brooding Italian aristocrat Maddalo (Byron) argues for despair. "We might be otherwise," Julian insists, "we might be all/we dream of: happy, high, majestical" were it not for our own "enchained" wills. To which Maddalo replies bitterly: "You talk utopia!"

That snap dismissal echoes down to our own day. We've been taught to fear utopian thinking, which is denounced as not only impractical but positively dangerous: the province of fanatics. In ignoring the lessons of history and the realities of human nature, utopian idealism results, inevitably, we are told, in dystopian outcomes. It's a modern version of the myth of Pandora's box: a warning against being too enquiring, too ambitious.

Fear of utopia, a mighty weapon in the arsenal of the ruling powers, has a long pedigree. Since Burke, at least, conservatives have warned that tampering with established institutions, encouraging people to expect too much, leads to disaster. The "failure" of every social experiment, from the French Revolution onward, is seized on as evidence of the perils of utopian thinking. Anti-utopianism was a staple of Cold War liberalism and was resuscitated as the "end of history" thesis following the collapse of the Soviet Union.

Increasingly we have been told that a utopian denial of realities lurks in even the most modest demands for regulation and redistribution. When it comes to the apparent dearth of alternatives, I'd argue that social democracy's long retreat into the arms of neo-liberalism is as great a factor as the demise of the Communist bloc.

While there are dangers in utopian thinking, the much greater danger is its absence. The reality is that we don't "talk utopia" nearly enough.

We need the attraction of a possible future as well as a revulsion at the actual present. If people are to make the sacrifices required by any struggle for social justice, then they need a bold and compelling idea of the world they're fighting for.

Utopian thinking is more than just model building: it is a critical tool, a means of interrogating present conditions. We have to exercise that supremely political faculty, the imagination, if we are not to be prisoners of a prevailing consensus.

Utopias provide a perspective from which the assumed limitations of the present can be scrutinised, from which familiar social arrangements are exposed as unjust, irrational or superfluous. You can't chart the surface of the earth, compute distances or even locate where you are without reference to a point of elevation — a mountain top, a star or satellite. Without utopias we enjoy only a restricted view of our own nature and capacities. We cannot know who we are.

We need utopian thinking if we are to engage successfully in the critical battle over what is or is not possible, if we are to challenge what are presented as immutable "economic realities". Without a clear alternative — the outlines of a just and sustainable society — we are forced to accept our opponent's parameters. We cede the definition of the possible to those with a vested interest in closing the aperture into a better future. The neo-liberal slogan *There is No Alternative* had to be answered by *Another World is Possible*, but we need to know and say much more about this other world.

In our utopian activity, let's learn from past errors. It's important to remember that a significant strand of utopianism, including Thomas More's book, is linked to western colonialism. This took many forms, from dreams of imposing a new order on ancient or (allegedly) empty lands (of which Zionism is a modern case) to Romantic and Orientalist fantasies.

In their critique of Utopian Socialism, Marx and Engels made two charges. First, that the method was wrong: a socialism imposed from above, reliant on altruistic benefactors. Second, that it was not sweeping enough, that it failed to recognise the need to replace the system as a whole.

Marx described communism as "the negation of the negation" — and our utopianism must remain at least in part a giant negation: of exploitation, inequality, greed, prejudice. Marx is criticised for not telling us more about what comes after the negation, but he did leave us with a still-vital guideline: *From each according to his/her ability, to each according to his/her need.*

Utopia is the good society, not the perfect society. A perfect society would be a static entity. Our utopia is one that is evolving, revising its goals and policies as circumstances change. It's an open, not a closed, system. Which means identifying its governing principles, its driving processes, may be more important than postulating fixed structures.

A utopia without dissent and argument is a nightmare. I don't want to belong to a community of interminable sweetness and harmony. In fact, argument will flower on a higher plane, grounded in a shared public domain to which all have real and equal access — politics in the best sense, with no professional politicians.

In our utopia the meaning of work will be transformed. There will be no more precious commodity than a person's time. "Choice" too will be redefined, salvaged from consumerism. There will be a deeper sense of ownership than the individualist version touted by the current system.

We cannot leave our utopian activity to think tanks. Nor should it be about some artificial "pre-figuration", an exercise in isolated purity. It has to involve getting your hands dirty: finding places for the utopian in the everyday and learning from the everyday the meaning of utopia.

We need to draw on the utopian elements in our midst. The NHS is far from perfect, but it operates under egalitarian principles deemed "utopian" in other fields and enjoys a significant degree of autonomy from the market, which makes it a kind of mini-utopia within British daily life — one reason the government is determined to destroy it.

We need to find ways to connect to the utopian yearnings that move millions of people, and which both the right wing and the advertising industry know too well how to exploit. We have to offer something more participatory, concrete and at the same time dynamic, more of a process, a journey, than an end product polished by the intelligentsia. In doing that, we can draw on a rich tradition going back to the Biblical prophets and found in almost every human society. In England alone, we can look to Langland, Winstanley, Thomas Spence, Ruskin, Morris and John Lennon — not forgetting More himself, in whose *Utopia* "gold is a badge of infamy".

Our utopia must imagine a new, humbler relationship between humans and their environment. The techno-utopias of the past with their dreams of total human mastery over nature now feel distinctly dystopic. On the other hand, the idea of an endlessly renewable energy source, a staple of science fiction, has moved from idle fantasy to urgent necessity. The climate change crisis is a good example of utopian thinking proving more realistic than its ostensibly pragmatic opponents. In the light of imminent catastrophe, utopia becomes common sense.

It is the anti-utopians who are guilty of arrogance and presumption in dismissing systematic alternatives as contrary to human nature (or economic "laws"). The utopians are more historically grounded. They know that capitalism had a beginning and will have an end. In contrast, neo-liberals practise the pejorative form of utopianism: imposing an abstract blueprint on the human species (and the planet), subordinating diverse human needs to the single compulsion of private profit. We are encouraged to entertain limitless, if narrowly defined, aspirations for ourselves as individuals, but our aspirations for our society are strictly ring-fenced. While it is held to be fatal to ignore economic realities, ecological realities can be indefinitely deferred. The anti-utopians who insist *There is No Alternative* end up denying the rest of us workable solutions to urgent problems.

The poets and prophets of the past gave us visions of a golden age of abundance, where the curse of labour had been lifted, where vines were laden with lustrous grapes, figs were like emeralds and streams gushed fresh water. Somehow, we need to find our own symbols of shared, sustainable abundance in a world starkly divided into rich and poor.

For William Blake, the work of utopia was a daily duty of the citizen. At the end of his *Vala* or *The Four Zoas*, he envisioned a world in which “the dark religions are departed and sweet science reigns”. It’s now up to us to imagine a world free of the dark religion of neo-liberalism, in which the sweet science of human solidarity prevails.

Early One Morning

Ken Worpole

The dead gull was lying on the seawall footpath, freshly eviscerated, its skeleton in the shape of a pair of angel's wings or the wings of Pegasus or Mercury: clearly the work of a peregrine falcon. We were indeed in J.M. Baker country, just a couple of miles east of Maldon on the River Blackwater in Essex on a May morning. Baker, the onlie begetter of peregrine poetics in the modern world, was a transport company manager who, in his spare time, cycled and walked the land between the Blackwater and the Crouch in homage to his adopted avenging angel. The recent re-publication of his lyrical writings on the Essex landscape have greatly helped raised the status of the county amongst Britain's naturalist and topographical elite.

Every few weeks or so, winter or summer, some friends and I walk the footpaths of coastal Essex. We are in search of nothing in particular, other than escaping from London to a world of large skies, shallow tides, mudflats, long-legged waders, dusty lanes and arable farmland, only an hour from Liverpool Street Station. Though we look for nothing we find much: traces of old holiday homes, caravans, wrecks of boats, rusty farm equipment deep in the grass, and on one occasion a large plastic jar containing cremated remains, labelled with name and time and place of committal, cast into the river unscattered, and caught in the tangle of a cluster of *aster maritima*: waterside Michaelmas Daisies.

Some older settlements still retain their original form and armature. One such is 'the Great Experiment' at Mayland, on the River Blackwater, a collection of abandoned outhouses, overgrown glasshouses, former railway tracks and river piers, located to the east of the more recent and flourishing settlement of Lower Mayland*. The original experiment was part of the wider Back to the Land movement which at the time involved the energies of Fabian Society principals such as George Lansbury, Joseph Rowntree and Joseph Fels. It was the latter member, Fels, who undertook the setting up of the Mayland colony, after meeting Thomas Smith, a former Manchester printer, who had already established a land-holding there in 1896. Fels subsequently bought 600 acres of farmland, which he divided up into 21 separate small-holdings, all to be made available to families wishing to start a new life away from the poverty of the city, and in some cases, from failed attempts to farm in the colonies, particularly Australia.

Fels himself was an American, of former Eastern European immigrants, who had inherited a fortune from the manufacture of soap and who had come to England to embrace the Fabian cause. He was already an avid follower of the land economist Henry George, and had previously joined George Lansbury in establishing a land colony for unemployed men at Hollesley Bay in Suffolk in 1887. As sometimes happens, over time this erstwhile utopian settlement changed hands, mutating into a prison farm for young male offenders (including Brendan Behan who based parts of his autobiographical novel, *Borstal Boy*, there). Latterly nick-named 'Holiday Bay' for its high number of escapes, it remains the largest prison farm in Britain, as well as being a unique stud farm for Suffolk Punch Horses, until very recently reared and groomed by the prisoners.

The transition from utopian experiment to prison farm is dismaying but not unexpected. It is clear when looking back to many similar utopian experiments in the 19th

---

*Most of what I know about 'the great experiment' at Mayland I found in Eileen Everitt's pamphlet, *The Development of Lower Mayland and Maylandsea during the 20th Century*, self-published, 2007, gratefully acknowledged.

and 20th centuries that an over-reliance on bricks, bonds and boundaries to shape and contain the visionary gleam, quickly produced a distancing relationship to the everyday world, with sanctuaries and utopian redoubts often retreating into isolationism and a sense of being at odds with the rest of society. The libertarian designer Stuart Brand warned against too easily eliding social ideas with architectural solutions, writing in his wonderful book, *How Buildings Learn*, that 'All buildings are predictions. All predictions are wrong.'

At Mayland, happily, this did not happen. Fels invited Thomas Smith to become the estate manager and gave him full rein in creating a viable self-sufficient economy. Smith was an enthusiast for what was then known as 'French gardening', involving the large-scale propagation of crops under glass, and he later wrote a book, *French Gardening*, which over time established his reputation. In 1950, by then an old man, he was awarded a gold medal by the Royal Horticultural Society.

Within a few years of setting up, the Mayland experiment was growing its own food, producing its own meat and dairy products, and providing homes and a school along with other social amenities for the colonists. Moreover, it was able to export produce to other parts of the region through the establishment of a short rail link to a tidal jetty, where boats could moor and set sail around the coast. The railway consisted of a small number of wooden trucks on bogies, pulled by horses — and at times by the workers themselves — carrying goods from The Homestead to the dock jetty. Visitors to the colony included Peter Kropotkin, Rider Haggard, Sidney & Beatrice Webb, Keir Hardie and Lansbury. The school had sliding side-panels to the single classroom so that in fine weather they could be drawn open, enabling the children to study in the fresh air.

The death of Fels in 1914, and the outbreak of the First World War, ended the experiment in its original form, though the community survived and a number of the plot-holders managed to buy their small-holdings and continue to make a living in the settlement. Some of the walnut trees survive as do many of the hawthorn hedges marking out the lanes and boundaries. The former railway track is now a straight dark tunnel of trees leading to an inlet on the River Blackwater. There are just enough remains to imagine the settlement as it was in its pioneering days, and to be glad that some people bettered their lives in this way.

The experiment at Mayland was no isolated affair. Land colonies of all persuasions were a feature of late Victorian religious enthusiasm and political idealism, and Essex, being close to the East End of London, was a home to many. Fels and Lansbury joined forces to create a farm colony for men from the Poplar workhouse and ex-soldiers in Laindon between 1904 and 1911. Laindon later became a pioneer of inter-war plotland self-build communities. At Ashingdon and Wickford, closer to Mayland, followers of Tolstoy established small-holding settlements in 1897 and 1898 respectively. Most famously, manufacturer F.H. Crittall built a model village in the modernist style for his workers at Silver End near Chelmsford in 1926, complete with farm, hotel, department store and sports centre. The settlement was entirely self-sufficient, with its own water supply and electricity generating scheme. In the 1930s Silver End was judged to be the healthiest village in Britain. The estate still stands.

The Salvation Army also created land colonies in Essex, the large one at Hadleigh established in 1891 surviving, today managed as an organic farm and a training centre for young people with disabilities. The Othona community at Bradwell-on-Sea continues to provide a spiritual retreat for all faiths and none, in a collection of chalets, originally established after the Second World War to bring British and German Christians together in a spirit of reconciliation. They also farm. The more you look for these 'experiments in living', the more you find.

Our walks often take us close by and sometimes through these scattered utopias, old and new. They are mostly unmarked on the map, but remain strong in people's memories and in a variety of local history pamphlets, memoirs, and social histories. Attachment to working the land, along with the physical benefits of life outdoors, seems to provide a powerful impulse behind many of these utopian schemes. From time to time we stop to talk to small-holders, river-boat dwellers, organic farmers and community activists in our walks, and it seems the impulse never goes away. The Essex landscape would be bereft without them.

Equal in Death: the Moravian Burial Ground

Gillian Darley

I pushed open a domestic-looking gate with a symbol of a lamb impressed on the metal, and found myself in a shady, sun-speckled garden, bluebells and late spring flowers dotted between the trunks of mature trees. A sundial stood sentinel at the end of the path and seats were sprinkled around it. Then I noticed, no more than whispering for attention at my feet, dozens of simply inscribed stone slabs laid flush on the ground.

The scene I remembered photographing some thirty-five years ago is the entrance to the Moravian burial ground at Fairfield, in Droylsden. Looking at the photograph again recently I can see no bluebells but the charm and intimacy of the scene I remembered is accurate. Returning, a few weeks ago, I found the gate and sundial still there, with the grass neatly mown to expose the gravestones and the trees now showing their age. Fairfield, the largest of the English Moravian settlements, was founded in 1785.

Owenite socialism and Fourierist utopianism spawned innumerable experiments in communal living in the early 19th century, flaring up and dying down like so many damp fireworks, leaving behind only vestigial traces, whether of fabric or their founding ideals. Among religious communities, Shaker settlements stand, deservedly admired for their extraordinary expression of lives ordered far beyond the norm, but the sect has gone. Celibacy was a self-fulfilling prophecy. Among replicable communal ventures only the Moravians have endured.

Fulneck, founded in 1748, was the first such in England. Mrs Philip Lybbe Powys, visiting in 1757, wrote in her journal, 'the situation is charming ... commanding the most delightful prospect.' Mrs Powys noticed three substantial buildings already completed on the side of the hill, 'the centre one is their chapel and house of their clergyman, in which he only and all their children constantly reside. The house on the one side is all for unmarried men, that on the other for the single Sisters, as 'tis call'd'. The school soon followed. Until they built more houses, married members of the community lived in the local village, Pudsey. As early as 1751, the Elders noted proudly that the beauty of their burial ground was often cited as 'the reason for deathbed requests for reception' into the Moravian Church. In every location their burial grounds became uncontrived places of calm and quiet beauty, there for the everyday pleasure of everyone. Even more than the carefully calibrated buildings, these gardens with their discreet recumbent stones represented a perfectly codified version of the Moravian communal society.

Its success depended on social and economic order. In many ways the Moravian community was the embodiment of what Arnold Wesker calls 'the energy of human aspiration' in the face of the ultimate impossibility of the utopian dream. The villages were carefully situated within striking distance of large markets for their goods (Fulneck to Leeds, Fairfield to Manchester, Gracehill, founded 1765, to Belfast). Economic self-sufficiency was the object while remaining respectful to the ties and obligations of a close (but not closed) community and existing family bonds. The practicality of the architecture and physical planning mirrored an essential conformity to a shared purpose — but not necessarily conformity in the eyes of the outside world. At Fulneck, visitors soon came to witness 'the oddness of their worship' and yet went away charmed by the place, the welcome they received, the grace of the women's dress and above all the glorious music, both instrumental and vocal, which greeted anyone who cared to attend their chapel on a Sunday.

Photo © Gillian Darley

The church of the Unitas Fratrum, the united brethren, had been 'renewed' in the 1720s, after almost two centuries of persecution. Herrnhut in Saxony was built on land given by Count Zinzendorf, a German landowner and soon to be leader of the congregation. From there, Moravian missionaries quickly fanned out around northern Europe, arriving in Greenland (to stay) by 1733. Every successive settlement was to begin as a regional variant on that original model — from Christiansfeld in Denmark to Bethlehem in Pennsylvania. At Fulneck, many of the earliest records list numerous German names suggesting that they too had been sent to Yorkshire from Herrnhut.

Moravian lives were determined by the church's organisation into 'choirs', the Elders, the leaders of these groups, being the only form of recognised seniority. Family bonds were important but choirs over-rode all. In chapel, women and men sat facing one another. The plan of most of the settlements emphasised an inward turned focus — Fairfield is virtually a square within a square — which looked towards their own occupations and observance, but also outwards. This pragmatic approach ensured their economic survival and had the benefit of attracting new members.

Moravian burial grounds were equally systematic. Just as the early 17th century botanic gardens attached to Padua, Leiden or Oxford universities depended upon geometry to display and relate taxonomies of species, so the Moravians divided their available land for burial between choirs. In death, everyone lay with his or her peers, rather than in families. The choirs of, respectively, married men and married women occupied two quarters of the ground, those of single men (and boys) and single women (and girls), the remaining two.

At Herrnhut they all lay on a hillside facing east, every individual under an identical stone slab with no more than a name and date inscribed. Zinzendorf's divine botanical garden had been planted against the Day of Resurrection. Lying there, in absolute equality, side by side, the congregation waited to rise again on the appointed hour. But there were to be a few notable exceptions. Count and Countess Zinzendorf chose prominence over equality, being buried in substantial vaults below their graves at Herrnhut. The Zinzendorf's former family tutor, David Nitschmann, who became the first bishop of the renewed Moravian church and who founded Bethlehem, Pennsylvania in 1741 followed suit, considering himself, in Craig Atwood's neat phrase, 'spiritual royalty in the midst of an egalitarian communal society.'

But the wider Moravian congregation believed in honourable unanimity in all things. They observed the egalitarian customs and norms of their own society, for example in their dress, 'plain to a degree yet pleasing' and while their contemporaries lived bound by a mesh of intricate social gradations and subtle measurements of class and condition, the Moravians — largely artisans — had effectively absolved themselves from all this in favour of equality in life and death. The Established church suggested that all became equal at death according to common law, but the pre-Victorian notion of universal citizenship in the churchyard was flexible at best. A site to the south of an Anglican church was preferable to one on the north, the latter designated for the less virtuous, and so on, with many uneasy variants.

Moravian burial ritual took place between the church hall and the burial ground, God's Acre, so that the earthly congregation moved calmly towards the heavenly. On Easter Sunday, the zenith of the Moravian church calendar, much of the service took place in the burial ground, remembering those who had died over the previous year and visiting family members.

When someone was nearing death, the congregation gathered to sing around the deathbed, and when that individual then 'fell asleep' (the preferred term) they were described as having gone 'home'. The burial within the choir system, rather than with the family, underlined the Moravian belief that they had already entered God's family. Funerals were predominantly musical affairs; a note from a trombone marked a death and the procession, from chapel to burial ground, was accompanied by the playing of cheerful music and choral singing. Everything conveyed a single optimistic message. The dead were simply awaiting new life. Mourning was discouraged. At Fairfield the sundial is inscribed, in decidedly matter of fact wording given the portent of the message, 'I die today, I live tomorrow'.

In complete contrast, Shaker celibacy and lack of belief in the Resurrection made the afterlife an irrelevancy, leaving their members indifferent to funerary rituals or the place of burial (graves were unmarked). Their society was itself a 'living building' and their settlements the ideal physical and organisational manifestation of precisely mirrored, but rigidly segregated, lives.

The image of a paradise garden, the spiritual dimension of a last resting place in a place approximating the Garden of Eden, proved enduringly potent. John Evelyn, a religious Englishman of conformist bent for whom the natural world, that of trees in particular, was divine, hoped to be buried in his own garden at Wotton in Surrey (though he was, in the end, buried in the family chapel attached to the parish church). The persuasive early 19th century arguments for urban garden cemeteries reinforced the imagery of a pastoral place of death, an eventual retreat from the city. But by allowing and even encouraging personal statements on a grandiloquent scale they would become overwhelmed by those trying to steal a march on their neighbours, even in death. No wonder, perhaps, that the Inspirationists, a radical North American offshoot from the German Moravians who had settled at Amana, Iowa, elected to lay out their burial ground on the usual principles but demarcated it with dour lines of cypresses, like heavily lined graph paper.

In every Moravian burial ground around the world each gravestone marked the life of a single member of the congregation, a standard measure of a body. That graphic egalitarianism surfaced briefly on an ambitious scale in Thomas Jefferson's Land Ordinance Act of 1785, (the Land Act of 1786). The even-handed parcelling of available land into 36 square mile townships, to be broken down into ever smaller square units until 'as few as possible ... be without at least a little portion of land' was an essentially democratic and socially just measure. It aimed to reward a free and hard-working people with land and in so doing provide an equitable measure of their aspiration and energy.

Equally, the Moravian burial ground, whether in Europe or the Americas, was a reflection of their shared beliefs and coherent guiding principles of a community. Only the rhythmic, elegiac formality of the early 20th century Commonwealth War Graves speaks to a similar ideal of equality in death, even if entirely at odds with the intensely hierarchical nature of the armed services in life.

Fairfield was built in 1785 after drawings signed by the 18-year-old son of the senior figure in the Moravian establishment in England. Ten years later, that young man, Benjamin Henry Latrobe, had become an experienced architect and engineer who in 1796 left Europe for North America, to take a leading role in building Thomas Jefferson's capital city. Briefly, the founding principles of a new nation and the patterns established by an idealistic, but well tested, community intersected.

My thanks to Lorraine Parsons, archivist at the Moravian Church Archives and Library, Muswell Hill, north London

Further Reading

Craig D. Atwood, *Community of the Cross; Moravian Piety in Colonial Bethlehem,* Philadelphia: University of Pennsylvania Press, 2004

Jorgen Boytler, *Moravian Values and Moravian Towns,* Christiansfeld, 2003

James Corner (with Alex MacLean), *Taking Measures across the American Landscape,* New Haven & London: Yale University Press, 1996

Gillian Darley, *Villages of Vision,* Nottingham: Five Leaves, 2007 (revised edition)

Adelaide L. Fries, *Customs and Practices of the Moravian Church,* Moravian Church in America, 1936, revised 2003

Dolores Hayden, *Seven American Utopias,* Cambridge, Mass.: MIT Press, 1976.

Mrs Philip Lybbe Powys, *Passages from the Diaries of Mrs Philip Lybbe Powys of Hardwick House, Oxon: A.D. 1756–1808,* 1899, online edition

C.H. Shawe, article in *Moravian Messenger,* March 1930

Ken Worpole, *Last Landscapes,* London: Reaktion Books, 2003

'Time and Tide Stay for No Man'
The Putney Debates, 1647–2012
John Payne

There has been a river crossing at Putney since medieval times, although the present stone structure is a mere 125 years old. The first wooden bridge was only built in 1729, before when the anxious traveller had to be content with a ferry boat across the swift-flowing tidal Thames. Now Putney Bridge is a vital link in London's creaking transport infrastructure. The travellers pass. A few may notice the stone churches at either end of the bridge — All Saints on the Fulham bank, St Mary's on the Putney bank. Fewer still will know of the symbolic role that St Mary's Putney has played in the evolution of ideas about democratic government. Bombed during the Second World War, and rebuilt since, crushed between the river, the busy High Street and the rather alarming block of flats that was once the home of International Computers Ltd., St Mary's Putney has seen life. And yet there are constants, as the words 'Time and Tide Stay for No Man' etched on the splendid sundial on the tower remind us. The restless tide ebbs and flows, our lives drain towards the sea. And still we attempt to maintain the illusion that somehow we are in control of our lives and destinies. And still we talk.

The Putney Debates of 1647 were not about Utopia. The men (we shall consider the women a little later) who met at St Mary's Putney in 1647 were, by and large, practical men. They were soldiers, the General Council of the Army, the supporters of Parliament in the struggle with the King — the English Civil War. Yet among them were some who indeed had Utopian visions. Men called Levellers, at first a term of abuse, later embraced; a term

Photo © John Payne

immediately recognisable to those who continue to believe in the moral repugnance of gross inequalities in wealth and life chances. Behind those few lay a Protestant religious and social ferment of millenarian proportions, of people confident enough, mad enough, to expect the imminent arrival of heaven on earth. The Thames flowed, indifferent, as it does today.

The basic document debated before, during and after the debates in St Mary's Church in 1647 is usually referred to as *An Agreement of the People*. It is not my purpose to enter into overmuch historical detail, and I have modernised spelling in every case. At the same time, the past is the past, is a different country and a different language too, and we do well to remember the remarkable amount of time spent during the 1647 debates in praying, and that many of the issues debated were internal to the army, such as the call for indemnity for events that had taken place during the war. The main demands were for equal representation in parliament, 'indifferently proportioned, according to the number of the inhabitants' (i.e. equal constituencies), and fixed term two-year parliaments elected on a fixed day in March, sitting from April to November. In addition, sovereignty was invested by the people in parliament, the powers of which were 'inferior only to theirs who choose them'. These powers include enacting laws, erecting offices and courts, appointing and dismissing officers and magistrates, making war and peace, dealing with foreign states.

Parliamentary democracy was not seen as a system in which the people ceded power to members of parliament, and here, one might say, lay the rub. Certain specific rights should be retained by the people themselves, such as religious belief and the right not to be conscripted into the army. Two important points were made about the rule of law. Firstly, there should be equality before the law: 'that no tenure, estate, charter, degree, birth, or place do confer any exemption from the ordinary course of legal proceedings'; secondly 'that as the laws ought to be equal, so they must be good, and not evidently destructive to the safety and well-being of the people'. Finally came the ringing declaration that 'These things we declare to be our native rights, and therefore are agreed and resolved to maintain them with our utmost possibilities against all opposition'. We hear the distant tones of the Declaration of Independence of the USA, and of all that has happened since, both good and bad, both question-answering and question-begging.

Power is vested, than, in both people and parliament. But who were these 'people'? There was much discussion at Putney of the 'unfree', of household servants for example. But more important for the future was the point of view of Cromwell and the other army grandees. They saw property as the link that tied individual people most closely to society and the state; therefore the ownership of a significant amount of property should define who participated, who voted, whose voice was heard. For the Levellers, the purpose of *An Agreement* was precisely that it was an 'agreement' — those who were enfranchised were those prepared to 'sign up' to a certain view of how the country should be run. Others (royalists, for example) placed themselves beyond the boundaries of the franchise. It was Thomas Rainborough, a representative of moderate Leveller opinion, who argued memorably for the voice of the propertyless poor to be heard in the affairs of state:

> ... for really I think that the poorest he that is in England has a life to live as the greatest he; and therefore truly, sir, I think it's clear that every man that is to live under a government ought first by his own consent to put himself under that government; and I do think that the poorest man in England is not at all bound in a strict sense to that government that he has not had a voice to put himself under.

In practice, the gradual extension of the franchise in the nineteenth and twentieth centuries owed much to the notion of a property-owning democracy, but in theory at least, it was quite incompatible with the view Rainborough put at Putney.

Rights have always been a thorny issue, complicated in the United Kingdom by our extraordinary adherence to the notion of 'subjects' rather than 'citizens'. It is all very well to have rights, but how can those rights be upheld in a manifestly unequal society? The case of the USA is instructive here. Enshrine rights in a written constitution and all will be well. Except that it wasn't. Black slaves did not have rights, and the bloody American Civil War was required to settle that issue. Civil Rights was just as difficult an issue and not until the 1950s was major progress made in that direction. Still, black people are over-represented among the urban poor, in the armed forces, in jail. No true equality, no true rights. Here in the UK, despite the incorporation of the European Declaration of Human Rights into UK law, there is still clamour for a Bill of Rights. Yet others think, as the Levellers thought, that only a living democracy and a vibrant civil society (our phrase, not theirs) can secure the people's rights. As Rainborough put it at Putney on 28 October 1647:

> I hear it said, 'It's a huge alteration, it's a bringing in of new laws', and that this kingdom has been under this government ever since it was a kingdom.
> If writings be true, there have been many scufflings between the honest men of England and those that have tyrannised over them; and if it be true what I have read, there is none of those just and equitable laws that the people of England are born to, but that they are entrenchments [= intrusions] altogether on the privileges once enjoyed by their rulers.
> But even if they were those which the people have been always under, if the people find that they are not suitable to freemen as they are, I know no reason to deter me, either in what I must answer before God or the world, from endeavouring by all means to gain anything that might be of more advantage to them than the government under which we live.

Included in 'rights', as Mary Wollstonecraft noted in her rejoinder to Thomas Paine's *Rights of Man*, were the rights of women. When Rainborough said 'the poorest he that is in England', it was not merely a verbal laziness.

He said 'he' and he meant 'he'. As Christopher Hill has shown in *The World Turned Upside Down*, it is in the pamphlet literature of the more radical of the Levellers, Diggers and Ranters, in the life and work of 'Honest John' Lilburne that we must search for any statement of sexual equality.

Ireton, Cromwell and other army grandees were defending the limitation of the vote to property owners. Rainsborough and his comrades were arguing that the distribution of property was in itself unfair, that it corresponded to conquest (the Norman Conquest specifically) and could and should be changed by law. They contrasted 'birthright' to 'property right'. It is the logic of this position that two years later took Gerard Winstanley and the Diggers to St George's Hill to lay claim to the land. For the Diggers, the 'just law' lay in their hearts rather than in any Act of Parliament.1649 was a year of defeat for the more radical voices within and beyond the army, as well as the year of the execution of King Charles. On 17 May, the ringleaders of a final rebellion by Leveller supporters within the army were executed at Burford, a pretty little Cotswold town. On 19 May the Commonwealth was established under Cromwell's rule. It was an ending of a sort.

And yet, and yet. Each year crowds are drawn to Burford in May to commemorate the Levellers and what they stood for. Leon Rosselson wrote his song 'The World Turned Upside Down' in which he remembered the Diggers in the sublimely utopian line: 'No man has any right to buy and sell the earth for private gain.' Tony Benn included a section on 'The Levellers and the English Democratic Tradition' in his seminal *Arguments for Socialism* (1979). So people remembered, finally, Putney. Here in the 1980s Labour politicians such as Tony Benn and Peter Hain (Putney candidate in 1983 and 1987) debated the future rather than the past. And here on 30/31 October 1997 the Quakers organised a weekend of celebration of the 350th anniversary of the original Putney Debates. The outlines of a new 'Agreement' were sketched and debated, a new agenda of environmental concern, economics for people not profit, and North-South solidarity. I sat there all weekend with my notebook and pencil, scribbling and remembering William Clarke, the recorder of the 1647 debates. It was the rediscovery and publication of his notebooks at the end of the nineteenth century which paved the way for the recognition of the importance of Putney, and musings over what it had meant and might still come to mean. I noted who was there, what claims they were making, whose voices were being heard. I noted that Vandana Shiva, who spoke, was one of the few non-white faces in the church. I noted the extraordinary claim by a group called 'The Jury' to represent 'the people of Putney'. Fat chance, I thought. People enjoyed the event and came back in 2007. No doubt it will not be the last time that a crowd gathers in Putney to debate the past, present and future of English democracy. Now there is a small, permanent exhibition in the church dedicated to the Putney Debates.

Back to 1997: a week later, I was in Putney Church again, this time for an academic debate about the significance and meaning of the Putney Debates. It was interesting. I understood that 1997 was not 1647, that people's view of the world had changed, that it was dangerous to demonise too strongly those who wanted change by slow and decided steps. I took the point that the Puritan groups convinced of their own truth and righteousness might be a dangerous foundation for any democracy. And yet when I look at my own home town, Frome in Somerset, and the surrounding villages, see the non-conformist chapels and meeting-houses closing, the visible presence of dissent and conflict within English society, I cannot help having still a sneaking regard for the Levellers and what they stood for, stood up for, and in some cases gave their lives for. There are people; there is power. There is memory; there is forgetting. We remember, we remember that we are many, that they (the rich and powerful) are few, we remember who we are and where we have come from.

We puzzle still about how liberty and equality might one day walk hand-in-hand. We can dream, we can imagine. But in the end it has to be asked whether imagination and dreams and utopias are enough. What about agency and action in the here and now in which we have been lucky or unlucky enough to live? We do not live in good times. As Marx asserted, we act, we make history, but not in times of our own choosing. Dream, imagine, yes. But it is the human spirit (imagination, courage, patience — and bloody hard work) that provides that crucial link between dream and action.

Further Reading

Philip Baker (compiler), introduction by Geoffrey Robertson *The Putney Debates: The Levellers*, London: Verso, 1997

Tony Benn (ed. Chris Mullin), *Arguments for Socialism,* London: Jonathan Cape, 1979

Christopher Hill, *The World Turned Upside Down: Radical Ideas During the English Revolution*, Harmondsworth: Penguin, 1972 (and subsequent editions)

Michael Mendle, *The Putney Debates of 1647: The Army, the Levellers, and the English State*, Cambridge: Cambridge University Press, 2001

A.S.P. Woodhouse (ed. and introduction, with foreword by A D Lindsay), *Puritanism and Liberty, Being the Army Debates (1647–9)*, London: J M Dent, 1938 (and subsequent editions).

See also

John Payne, *Journey up the Thames: William Morris and modern England*, Nottingham: Five Leaves Publications, 2000, chapter 3

http://www.putneydebates.com

A Factory as it Might Be
William Morris

We socialists are often reproached with giving no details of the state of things which would follow on the destruction of that system of waste and war which is sometimes dignified by the lying title of the harmonious combination of capital and labour. Many working people say "We admit that the present system has produced unsatisfactory results, but at least it is a system; you ought to be able to give us some definite idea of the results of that reconstruction which you call Socialism."

To this Socialists answer, and rightly, that we have not set ourselves to build up a system to please our tastes, nor are we seeking to impose it on the world in a mechanical manner, but rather that we are assisting in bringing about a development of history which would take place without our help, but which, nevertheless, compels us to help it; and that, under these circumstances, it would be futile to map out the details of life in a condition of things so different from that in which we have been born and bred.

Those details will be taken care of by the men who will be so lucky as to be born into a society relieved of the oppression which crushes us, and who surely will be, not less, but more prudent and reasonable than we are. Nevertheless, it seems clear that the economical changes which are in progress must be accompanied by corresponding developments of men's aspirations; and the knowledge of their progress cannot fail to rouse our imaginations into picturing for ourselves that life at once happy and manly which we *know* social revolution will put within the reach of all men.

Of course the pictures so drawn will vary according to the turn of mind of the picturer, but I have already tried to show in *Justice** that healthy and undomineering individuality will be fostered and not crushed out by Socialism. I will, therefore, as an artist and as handicraftsman venture to develop a little the hint contained in *Justice,* of April 12th, 1884, on the conditions of pleasant work in the days when we shall work for livelihood *and pleasure* and not for "profit."

Our factory, then, is a pleasant place — no very difficult matter when, as I have said before, it is no longer necessary to gather people into miserable, sweltering hordes for profit's sake — for all the country is in itself pleasant, or is capable of being made pleasant with very little pains and forethought. Next, our factory stands amidst gardens as beautiful (climate aside) as those of Alcinous, since there is no need of stinting it of ground, profit rents being a thing of the past, and the labour on such gardens is like enough to be purely voluntary, as it is not easy to see the day when 75 out of every 100 people will not take delight in the pleasantest and most innocent of occupations, and our working people will assuredly want open-air relaxation from their factory work. Even now, as I am told, the Nottingham factory hands could give many a hint to professional gardeners in spite of all the drawbacks of a great manufacturing town. One's imagination is inclined fairly to run riot over the picture of beauty and pleasure offered by the thought of skilful cooperative gardening for beauty's sake, which beauty would by no means exclude the raising of useful produce for the sake of livelihood.

"Impossible," I hear an anti-Socialist say. My friend, please to remember that most factories sustain today large and handsome gardens, and not seldom parks and woods of many acres in extent; with due appurtenances of highly paid Scotch professional gardeners, wood reeves, bailiffs, gamekeepers, and the like, the whole being

*The newspaper of the Social-Democratic Federation

managed in the most wasteful way conceivable; *only* the said gardens, etc., are twenty miles away from the factory, *out of the smoke,* and are kept up for *one member of the factory only,* the sleeping partner to wit, who may, indeed, double that part by organising its labour (for its own profit) in which case he receives ridiculously disproportionate pay additional.

Well, it follows in this garden business that our factory must make no sordid litter, befoul no water, nor poison the air with smoke. I need say nothing more on that point as, "profit" apart, it would be easy enough.

Next, as to the buildings themselves, I must ask to say something, because it is usually supposed that they must of necessity be ugly, and truly they are almost always at present mere nightmares; but it is, I must assert, by no means necessary that they should be ugly, nay, there would be no serious difficulty in making them beautiful, as every building might be which serves its purpose duly, which is built generously as regards material, and which is built with pleasure by the builders and designers; indeed, as things go, those nightmare buildings aforesaid sufficiently typify the work they are built for, and look what they are: temples of overcrowding and adulteration and over-work, of unrest, in a word; so it is not difficult to think of our factory buildings, showing on their outsides what they are for, reasonable and light work, cheered at every step by hope and pleasure. So in brief, our buildings will be beautiful with their own beauty of simplicity as workshops, not bedizened with tomfoolery as some are now, which do not any the more for that hide their repulsiveness; but moreover, besides the mere workshops, our factory will have other buildings which may carry ornament further than that, for it will need dining-hall, library, school, places for study of different kinds, and other such structures; nor do I see why, if we have a mind for it, we should not emulate the monks and craftsmen of the Middle Ages in our ornamentation of such buildings;

why we should be shabby in housing our rest and pleasure and our search for knowledge, as we may well be shabby in housing the shabby life we lead now.

And, again, if it is doubted as to the possibility of getting these beautiful buildings on the score of cost, let me once again remind you that every great factory does today sustain a palace (often more than one) amidst that costly garden and park aforesaid out of the smoke, but that this palace, stuffed as it is with all sorts of costly things, is for one member of the factory only, the sleeping partner — useful creature! It is true that the said palace is mostly, with all it contains, beastly ugly, but this ugliness is but a part of the bestial waste of the whole system of profit-mongering, which refuses cultivation and refinement to the workers, and, therefore, can have no art, not even for all its money.

So we have come to the outside of our factory of the future, and seen that it does not injure the beauty of the world, but adds to it rather. I will try to give a picture of how the work goes on there.

We have in previous pages tried to look through the present into the future, and see a factory as it might be, and got as far as the surroundings and outside of it; but the externals of a true palace of industry can only be realised naturally and without affection by the work which is to be done in them being in all ways reasonable and fit for human beings; I mean no mere whim of some one rich and philanthropic manufacturer will make even one factory permanently pleasant and agreeable for the workers in it; he will die or be sold up, his heir will be poorer or more single-hearted in his devotion to profit, and all the beauty and order will vanish from the short-lived dream; even the external beauty in industrial concerns must be the work of society and not of individuals.

Now as to the work, first of all it will be useful, and, therefore, honoured; because there will be no temptation to make mere useful toys, since there will be no rich men cudgelling their brains for means for spending superfluous money, and consequentially no "organisers of labour" pandering to degrading follies for the sake of profit, wasting their intelligence and energy in contriving snares for cash in the shape of trumpery which they themselves heartily despise. Nor will the work turn out trash; there will be no millions of poor to make a market for wares which no one would choose to use if he were not driven to do so; everyone will be able to afford things good of their own kind, and, as will be shown hereafter, will have knowledge of goods enough to reject what is not excellent; course and rough wares may be made for rough and temporary purposes, but they will openly proclaim themselves for what they are; adulteration will be unknown.

Furthermore, machines of the most ingenious and best-approved kinds will be used when necessary, but will be used simply to save human labour; nor, indeed, could they be used for anything else in such well-ordered work as we are thinking about; since, profit being dead, there would be no temptation to pile up wares whose apparent value as articles of use, their conventional value as such, does not rest on the necessities or reasonable desires of men for such things, but on artificial habits forced on the public by the craving of the capitalists for fresh and ever fresh profit; these things having no real value as things to be used, and their conventional (let us say sham) utility value has been the breed of their value, as articles of exchange for profit, in a society founded on profit-mongering.

Well, the manufacture of useless goods, whether harmful luxuries for the rich or disgraceful make-shifts for the poor, having come to an end, and we still being in possession of the machines once used for mere profit-grinding, but now used only for saving human labour, it follows that much less labour will be necessary from each workman; all the more as we are going to get rid of all non-workers, and busy-idle people; so that the working time of each member of our factory will be very short, say, to be much within the mark, four hours a day.

Now, next it may be allowable for an artist — that is, one whose ordinary work is pleasant and not slavish — to hope that in no factory will all the work, even that necessary four hours' work, be mere machine-tending; and it follows from what has been said above about machines being used to save labour, that there would be no work which would turn man into mere machines; therefore, at least some portion of the work, the necessary and in fact compulsory work I mean, would be pleasant to do; the machine-tending ought not to require a very long apprenticeship, therefore in no case should any one person be set to run up and down after a machine through all his working hours every day, even so shortened as we have seen; now the attractive work of our factory, that which was pleasant in itself to do, would be of the nature of art; therefore all slavery of work ceases under such a system, for whatever is burdensome about the factory would be taken turn and turn about, and so distributed, would cease to be a burden — would be, in fact, a kind of rest from the more exciting or artistic work.

Thus, then, would the sting be taken out of the factory system, in which, as things now are, the socialisation of labour, which ought to be a blessing to the community, has been turned into a curse by the appropriation of the products of its labour by individuals, for the purpose of gaining for them the very doubtful advantages of a life of special luxury, and often of mere idleness; the result of which, to the mass of the workers, has been a dire slavery, of which long hours of labour, ever-increasing strain of labour during those hours, and complete repulsiveness in the work itself have been the greatest evils.

It remains for me to set forth my most sanguine hopes of the way in which the gathering together of people in such social bodies as properly-ordered factories might be, may be utilised for increasing the general pleasure of life, and raising its standard, material and intellectual; for creating, in short, that life rich in incident and variety, but free from the strain of mere sordid trouble, the life which the individualist vainly babbles of, but which the Socialist aims at directly, and will one day attain to.

In a duly ordered society, in which people would work for a livelihood, and not for the profit of another, a factory might not only be pleasant as to its surroundings, and beautiful in its architecture, but even the rough and necessary work done in it might be so arranged as to be neither burdensome in itself nor of long duration for each worker; but, furthermore, the organisation of such a factory, that is to say of a group of people working in harmonious cooperation towards a useful end, would of itself afford opportunities for increasing the pleasure of life.

To begin with, a factory will surely be a centre of education; any children who seem likely to develop gifts towards its special industry would gradually and without pain, amidst their book-learning be drawn into technical instruction which would bring them at last into a thorough apprenticeship for their craft; therefore, the bent of each child having been considered in choosing its instruction and occupation, it is not too much to expect that children so educated will look forward eagerly to the time when they will be allowed to work at turning out real useful wares; a child whose manual dexterity has been developed without undue forcing side by side with its mental intelligence would surely be as eager to handle shuttle, hammer or what not for the first time as a real workman, and begin making, as a young gentleman now is to get hold of his first gun and begin killing.

This education so begun for the child will continue for the grown man, who will have every opportunity to practice the niceties of his craft if he be so minded, to carry it to the utmost degree of perfection, not for the purpose of using his extra knowledge and skill to sweat his fellow-workman, but for his own pleasure and honour as a good artist. Similar opportunities will be afforded him to study, as deeply as the subject will bear, the science of his craft is founded; besides, a good library and help in studying it will be provided by every productive group (or factory), so that the worker's other voluntary work may be varied by the study of general science or literature.

But, further, the factory could supply another educational want by showing the general public how its goods are made. Competition being dead and buried, no new process, no detail of improvements in machinery would be hidden from the first inquirer; the knowledge which might thus be imparted would foster a general interest in work, and in the realities of life, which would surely tend to elevate labour and create a standard of excellence in manufacture, which in its turn would breed a strong motive towards exertion in the workers.

A strange contrast such a thing would be to that now existing! For today the public, and especially that part of it which does not follow any manual occupation, is grossly ignorant of crafts and processes, even when they are carried out at their own doors; so that most of the middle class are not only defenceless against the most palpable adulterations, but, also, which is far more serious, are of necessity whole worlds removed from any sympathy from the life of the workshop.

So managed, therefore, the factory, by co-operation with other industrial groups will provide an education for its own workers, and contribute its share to the education of citizens outside, but, further, it will, as a matter of course, find it easy to provide for more restful amusements, as it will have ample buildings for library, schoolroom, dining-hall and the like; social gatherings, musical or dramatic entertainments will obviously be easy to manage under such conditions.

One pleasure — and that a more serious one — I must mention, a pleasure which is unknown at present to the workers, and which, even for the classes of ease and leisure, only exists in a miserably corrupted and degraded form, I mean the practice of the fine arts. People living under the conditions of life above-mentioned, having manual skill, technical and general education, and leisure to use these advantages, are quite sure to develop a love of art, that is to say, a sense of beauty and an interest in life, which in the long run must stimulate them to the desire for artistic creation, the satisfaction of which is of all pleasures the greatest.

I have started by supposing our group of social labour busying itself in the production of bodily necessaries; but we have seen that such work will only take a small part of each worker's time; their leisure, beyond mere bodily rest and recreation, I have supposed would employ in perfecting themselves in the niceties of their craft, or in research as to its principles; some would stop there, others would take to studying more general knowledge, but some — and I think most — would find themselves impelled towards the creation of beauty, and would find their opportunities for this under their hands as they worked out their due quota of necessary work for the common good; these would amuse themselves by ornamenting the wares they made, and would only be limited in the quantity and quality of such work by artistic considerations as to how much or what kind of work really suited the wares; nor, to meet a possible objection, would there be any danger of such ornamental work degenerating into mere amateur twaddle, such as is now inflicted on the world by ladies and gentlemen in search for a refuge from boredom; because our workers will be thoroughly educated as workers and will know well what good work and true finish (not trade finish) means, and because the public, being a body of workers also, everyone in some line or other, will well understand what real work means. Our workers, therefore, will do their artistic work under keen criticism of themselves, their workshop comrades, and a public composed of intelligent workmen.

To add beauty to their necessary daily work will furnish outlet for the artistic aspirations of most men;

but, further, our factory which is externally beautiful, will not be inside like a clean jail or workhouse; the architecture will come inside in the form of such ornament as may be suitable to the special circumstances. Nor can I see why the highest and most intellectual art, pictures, sculpture, and the like should not adorn a true place of industry. People living a manly and reasonable life would have no difficulty in refraining from overdoing both these and other adornments: here then would be opportunities for using the special talents of the workers, especially in cases where the daily necessary work affords scanty scope for artistic work.

Thus our Socialistic factory, besides turning out goods useful to the community will provide for its own workers work light in duration, and not oppressive in kind, education in childhood and youth, serious occupation, amusing relaxation and more rest for the leisure of the workers, and withal that beauty of surroundings, and the power of producing beauty which are sure to be claimed by those who have leisure, education and serious occupation.

No one can say that such things are not desirable for the workers, but we Socialists are striving to make them seem not only desirable but necessary, well knowing that under the present system of society they are impossible of attainment — and why? Because we cannot afford the time, trouble, and thought necessary to obtain them. Again, why cannot we? *Because we are at war,* class against class, and man against man; all our time is taken up with that; we are forced to busy ourselves not with the arts of peace, but with the arts of war, which are, briefly, trickery and oppression. Under such conditions of life, labour can but be a terrible burden, degrading to the workers, more degrading to those who live upon their work. This is the system which we seek to overthrow and supplant by one in which labour will no longer be a burden.

The Factory We Never Had

Colin Ward

As the decades roll by, it becomes more and more evident that the truly creative socialist thinker of the nineteenth century was not Karl Marx, but William Morris. His most eminent Marxist biographer, the late E.P. Thompson, virtually admitted this when he came to revise his massive volume *William Morris: Romantic to Revolutionary.*[1] When it first appeared in 1955, critics complained that it was a great Stalinist steam-roller, flattening Morris into a cardboard cut-out of a card-carrying Communist Party member.

Maybe it was that, but it was a great deal more beside, and in his postcript to the later version, Thompson explained that "Morris, by 1955, had claimed me. My book was by then, I suppose, already a work of muffled 'revisionism'. The Morris/Marx argument has worked inside me ever since. When, in 1956, my disagreements with orthodox Marxism became fully articulate, I fell back on modes of perception which I'd learned in those years of close company with Morris, and I found, perhaps, the will to go on arguing from the pressure of Morris behind me."

It was a namesake of his, Paul Thompson, who wrote the best of all accounts of Morris, *The Work of William Morris,* first published in 1967 and reprinted several times since then.[2] What does it matter, he asks, whether Morris was a romantic, an anarchist, a Marxist, or even a crypto-Fabian? The important thing is that he had a world view of extraordinary richness, which again and again foreshadows our own preoccupations: "the destruction by the international economy, not just of ancient cultures, but of the natural resources and ecology of the earth itself; the crippling of local independence by spreading centralisation and bureaucracy, the stifling of natural creativity and zest for learning of children by institutionalised schooling; the cramming of working people into barrack-like housing..."

But beyond this relevance, for Paul Thompson there is a special reason for Morris's importance for us: his remarkable anticipation of the problems posed to socialists within a late-twentieth century consumer society: "Socialism was originally the product of the age of the factory, and it bears that mark in its primary focus upon work. This is a major reason why socialism has always had a more direct appeal to men than to women, and equally why, with the growth of leisure and a home-centred way of life, its significance to ordinary life has become less and less obvious. But Morris stands alone among major socialist thinkers in being as concerned with housework and the home as with work in the factory. The transformation of both factory and home was equally necessary for the future fulfilment of men and women. Morris wanted everyday life as a whole to become the basic form of creativity, of art: 'For a socialist, a house, a knife, a cup, a steam engine, must be either a work of art, or a denial of art.'"

Morris's account of A *Factory As It Might Be* comes from 1884, one of the busiest years of an endlessly busy life. He was writing week by week in *Justice,* the organ of the Social-Democratic Federation, founded in January of that year, and in December had resigned, with a majority of the Executive, to form the Socialist League. But all through that year he was also lecturing in English and Scottish cities and towns with a series of topics, some of which became famous. E.P. Thompson records that the main themes he was offering at this time were "Useful Work versus Useless Toil", "Art and Labour", "Misery and the Way Out", and "How We Live and How We Might Live." He explains that "These lectures, with great variety of illustration and vigour of expression, followed a similar pattern. First Morris examined, in some fresh and striking manner, the reality of life and labour in capitalist society. Next, he presented by contrast the vision of true society, creative and responsive to beauty, and called his listeners to action in the struggle to achieve this vision."

The factory of his vision is a handsome group of buildings, surrounded by gardens, cultivated co-operatively "for beauty's sake, which beauty would by no means exclude the raising of useful produce for the sake of livelihood." And he notes that "the Nottingham factory hands could give many a hint to professional gardeners". He is right. The rose-grower Harry Wheatcroft recalls how in the 19th century Dean Hole, "the man who really transformed rose-growing in Britain", estimated that every third family in Nottingham had an allotment garden. Morris's factory would combine work and leisure with technical education, would have its nursery, school, restaurant and concert hall. It would be adorned with painting and sculpture. It would be a neighbourhood's social centre and the place where children learned by doing. His account of the factory also refutes those critics who, a century after his death, still dismiss Morris as a medievalist dreamer, an anachronism in the machine age, for he argues that "machines of the most ingenious and best-approved kinds will be used when necessary, but will be used simply to save human labour", so that the working hours will be reduced to about four hours a day.

As for the tedium of repetitive work, he observes that "the machine tending ought not to require a very long apprenticeship, therefore in no case should any one person be set to run up and down after a machine through all his working hours every day" since, apart from the reduction of working time, "whatever is burdensome about the factory would be taken turn in turn about, and so distributed, would cease to be a burden — would be, in fact, a kind of rest from the more exciting or artistic work."

Here Morris is anticipating the findings of highly-paid industrial psychologists a century later. Plenty of us find a repetitive task restful, provided that everyone else shares it and provided that it occupies a short amount of our working day. The whole tragedy of monotonous jobs on the assembly line, whether it is actually a line or a draughty shed where women gut chickens all day for the food-processing industry, is that the more hours they can get, the happier they are, simply for the sake of a pathetically small pay-packet.

So what became of Morris's factory vision? Several industrialists set about creating "model" factories. Eleven years after Morris's essay, George Cadbury moved his chocolate factory to Bournville outside Birmingham, where, the historian Gillian Darley explains, "The factory was surrounded by gardens, where the white-gowned workers could idle by the rose bushes in their lunch breaks; another palliative for the tedium of assembly-line work."[3] And even earlier, in 1888, when William Hesketh Lever moved his factory to Port Sunlight, he explained that he wanted his workers to "learn that there is more enjoyment in life than the mere going to and returning from work and looking forward to Saturday night to draw their wages." But Gillian Darley quotes a trade unionist's comment that "no man of an independent turn of mind could breathe for long in the atmosphere of Port Sunlight".

The tradition of the model factory persisted. Studying the lives of two tragic sisters, Alexandra Artley found that their happiest days were the ten years they worked for Courtaulds Red Scar rayon works outside Preston from 1970 to 1980. "Going to Courtaulds was like a holiday camp to us." In her book *Murder in the Heart* (Hamish Hamilton, 1993), Alexandra Artley drew upon their Morris-like recollections of breakfast at Courtaulds; "...here, from the largesse of a good employer, they could choose and choose and eat and eat the most delicious hot subsidised things they were denied at home... the warmth of the vast room with windows steamy against a frosty northern day, committed cooks in absolutely spotless white aprons and caps, and the long, under-heated chrome counters, subtly lighting trays of crisply fried bacon, big round sausages, glistening fried eggs, kidneys, golden triangles of fried bread, hot buttery toast, well-grilled tomatoes so sweetly squidgy in the middle, and gallons and gallons of hot, sweet tea. "Oh," said June, looking back on the vast hungers of youth, "the breakfasts at Courtaulds were *lovely*!'"

This sensual account is a reminder that what made factory work acceptable to millions, apart from the pay-packet, were incidentals, like the company of fellow workers, not a concern for the product. But if you travel in Morris's footsteps through industrial Britain in the 1990s you are overwhelmed by dereliction. Statistically, through the shift of manufacture from Europe and North America to the countries of the Pacific Rim or Latin America, where labour costs are cheaper, the owners of capital have shifted production, while automation and a change in the materials used have made the factory itself obsolete. Capital has achieved its object which was to eliminate labour. When Alexandra Artley sought out the sight of those enormous breakfasts, she found that "What had once been Courtaulds rayon mill now seemed to be something very different and a huge board at the foot of the drive stated the names of 'companies on site'. They seemed to be very 1980s-sounding names, such as Assembly Line Recording Studio, Windowland North-West and Bodycare Toiletries Ltd... there was no rayon works any more — just smart new, grey metal factories." A handful of socially-conscious capitalists may have taken notice of Morris's industrial ideal, but have gradually abandoned it because industrial welfare added to the cost of production, by comparison with that of poor countries. And yet another of Morris's demands has been completely lost. He thought that "the factory could supply another educational want by showing the general public how its goods are made". This comment anticipated the principle that, generations later, the American anarchist

Paul Goodman called the "transparency of operation", the idea that we should all be able to understand the functioning of the industrial products we use every day. But every item of electronic equipment in our homes has a label that warns "No user serviceable parts inside."

It was Morris's contemporary and friend Peter Kropotkin who added some thoroughly modern contributions to his comments on industrial production. In his study of *Fields, Factories and Workshops* of 1899, he gathered a mass of statistical evidence to show that ideologists of both right and left had exaggerated the scale of factory production. Most of our ordinary daily needs were produced in a small-workshop economy. And he anticipated the changes in sources of motive power that in the 20th and 21st centuries would make the large factory obsolete. We see this in the obsolescence all around us today.

This does not mean that Morris's vision of a factory as it might be has no significance for the future. It simply means that we have failed to achieve the humanisation of work that was at the heart of his life's ambition to separate useful work from useless toil.

---

[1] William Morris, *Romantic to Revolutionary,* 2nd revised edition, Merlin Press, 2011

[2] Paul Thompson, *The Work of William Morris,* Heinemann, 1967

[3] Gillian Darley, *Villages of Vision,* Architectural Press, 1975, new edition, Five Leaves, 2007

[4] Peter Kropotkin, *Fields, Factories and Workshops,* Freedom Press, 1998

News from Nowhere

Mandy Vere

On Mayday 1974, Bob Dent was struggling to open the door to a small shop premises on Manchester Street, Liverpool. The key wouldn't work. It was the opening day for News from Nowhere (NfN) and it looked like a disaster. Luckily he soon realised the key was merely upside down, and the life of an iconic radical bookshop began.

Bob had been a student activist at LSE with Maggie Wellings; together they decided to return to Liverpool and for Bob to start a radical bookshop in the mould of London's Rising Free. It was to be non-sectarian, broadly libertarian and provide books and pamphlets unavailable elsewhere. With a loan from Maggie's Liverpool Chinese family, the dream was realised, taking the name from William Morris's utopian novel. Little would they have realised not how many further trials the bookshop would endure, but how enduring it would become. NfN outlived nine other radical bookshops in Liverpool, more than a hundred radical bookshops nationwide, and survived the decimation of the independent booktrade.

The stock ranged from left critiques of the Soviet Union to anti-imperialist struggles from Latin America to Ireland, from the *Little Red Schoolbook* to R.D. Laing and Wilhelm Reich. You would have been hard-pressed to find such works in mainstream bookshops at the time and there was a ready audience among the left in Liverpool. In those early days 1,000 titles were stocked and takings were around £150 a week, kept in a biscuit tin. Wages were taken out of the tin as necessary. When Mandy Vere joined in 1976, the feminist emphasis increased with Kate Millett, Germaine Greer and Shulamith Firestone appearing on the shelves. Six copies a week of *Gay News* were stocked. The shop was crammed with subversive literature and the staff had to squeeze onto a bench in the window to work. The *Liverpool Free Press*, an investigative, campaigning newspaper started by ex-*Liverpool Echo* journalists, including Brian Whitaker (who later joined the *Guardian*), had a tiny office upstairs. It was an influential paper, at one point credited with bringing down the local Council in Kirkby by exposing corruption over building contracts awarded to councillors' cronies.

In 1977 News from Nowhere moved to a much larger, but extremely dilapidated, building round the corner in Whitechapel. At last there was room to expand. A massive range of cheap, agitprop pamphlets took over the whole back wall; anti-sexist, anti-racist children's books appeared; a group of old sofas and a kettle for tea-making were introduced, in the tradition of revolutionary coffee houses. Books were imported from America, especially those exciting new feminist authors, and a range of LPs were stocked, by musicians such as Leon Rosselson, and women blues singers. Exhibitions were held, including paintings of Gramsci, and Don McCullin's photographs from *The Palestinians* by Jonathan Dimbleby, and Literary Lunches featuring local historian Alan O'Toole (one of the discoverers of Robert Tressell's pauper's grave in Liverpool) as well as members of Unity Theatre and local writers' workshops. Booklists were produced using the tried and tested Gestetner duplicator. Younger people can hardly imagine the laborious and messy nature of typing stencils, correcting mistakes with pink fluid, and inking the drum to run off leaflets.

The sofas attracted many a character. There was "Peter the Great" who loved the sound of his own voice;

an eccentric Stalinist, Dr May, who carried a rolled-up umbrella and harangued anyone careless enough to sit down for a quiet read; and the old anarchist Bob who, during a period of homelessness, would wash his smalls in the back sink and hang them over the gas fire.

Meanwhile the stock expanded along with the radical publishing world. Pluto, Zed and Verso were all now well-established. Virago, Women's Press and smaller feminist presses such as Sheba and Onlywomen were publishing exciting lists and gay publishers such as Gay Men's Press and Brilliance Books were emerging. In 1989 the *Radical Bookseller* produced a list of four hundred radical publishers, and a year later a list of 130 radical bookshops. The range of feminist magazines alone was impressive: *Spare Rib*, *Red Rag*, *Women's Report*, *Shrew*, *Trouble & Strife*, *Scarlet Women* and, for young women, *Shocking Pink*. A radical distribution company was established — the Publications Distribution Co-operative. The Federation of Alternative Booksellers, which became the Federation of Radical Booksellers, had sixty-odd members and twice yearly meetings. So there was a ready-made network of outlets for radical publications and News from Nowhere was part of this movement. The bookshop was also an active partner in local campaigns such as the National Abortion Campaign, Troops Out and the anti-nuclear movement. The shop was centrally involved with the alternative political and social club, Liberty Hall, which met every Sunday night, hosting left theatre groups, films, debates and music.

Then, in 1979, Mandy was sentenced to six months in prison for importation of cannabis, due to a parcel being addressed c/o the bookshop. As "Mandy is Innocent" was spray-painted around the city, more workers had to be drafted in to help run the shop and the beginning of the women's collective was formed as Denise and Madeleine joined. The working practice had always been a collective but it was decided to register as a Workers' Co-operative and move from the biscuit-tin approach to properly audited accounts. And so News from Nowhere Co-operative was established in 1984. When Bob left to pursue a career in journalism the collective consciously became women-only. The Women's Liberation Movement was in full swing and the bookshop wanted to enable women to acquire skills in bookselling and business, and to enjoy the positive aspects of working autonomously in a women-only group. They saw a difference between separatism,

Photo © News from Nowhere

whereby women attempted to live separately from men in closed communities and political organisations, and autonomy, whereby women operated within a mixed context but were autonomous from men, supporting each other and making their own decisions.

This was a time when some customers and trade reps would take one look at the woman behind the till and ask to see the boss, or even address their query to a male customer standing nearby rather than believe women could be in charge. The collective received a lot of criticism from socialists at the time, but there is a point of view which contends that the survival of News from Nowhere is due in part to this courageous decision. Certainly the number of women who have worked or volunteered in the shop, benefiting from participation and training, must now be close to a hundred. Feminist campaigns were in the forefront of the Federation of Radical Booksellers too. There was a meeting of Women in Bookselling, and an influential campaign against sexism in publishing when Susie Orbach's *Fat is a Feminist Issue* was published with a sexist image on the cover. Stickers were produced to encourage book-buyers to write to publishers to complain about such covers. Along with feminist publishers, women in radical bookshops were a force to be reckoned with in the booktrade and arguably helped bring an end to some of the more blatant forms of sexism.

As Liverpool entered the 1980s, Margaret Thatcher was in power and the next decade would see the bookshop living through the Thatcher years, with difficulty, but, like the rest of the city, with determination. Just as the Toxteth Uprisings were happening in Liverpool 8, a campaign of arson, violence and intimidation was starting against numerous radical bookshops throughout the country, News from Nowhere becoming one of the worst hit. For a period of six to eight years, attacks came in waves, quite often weekly, if not daily. Gangs of fascist men, identifying themselves via stickers and leaflets as the

National Socialist Party of the UK, would target the bookshop on a Saturday, knocking over shelving units, smashing windows and, on occasion, assaulting members of staff and customers. But by far the worst problem was a series of arson attacks at night. At least six were recorded, some more serious than others, but none managing to completely destroy the shop. There would be damage to the window, where the fascists had prised off the wooden shutters, but the worst damage to the books was usually caused by the fire brigade's water hoses. The police were of no use, never arriving until too late, and treating bookshop staff as part of a political conflict between left and right. Only one minor case ever reached court. Besides, the bookshop always had an ambivalent attitude to the police since Mandy's imprisonment and in the context of police brutality towards the Black community. As always, the best support was from friends and supporters in progressive movements. Liverpool 8 community leaders came down to show support and the other radical bookshops locally and nationally did what they could to publicise the situation. Local supporters, known as the Conspirators, rallied round to help practically, raising the funds to equip the shop with steel shutters. This kept the women staff extremely fit, taking thirteen steel shutters on and off every day! Friends also filled the shop on Saturdays, and even stayed overnight. But at least a couple of workers resigned as the strain of those days became unbearable. There would not have been many job descriptions which required an ability to deal with fascist attacks. The location of the shop was a problem as it was isolated from other shops, next to a derelict site. The collective would spend until 1989 searching for alternative premises on the other side of town.

Meanwhile, throughout the eighties, there was the Falklands War, the Miners' Strike, Greenham Common, the Irish war against British occupation and mass unemployment to deal with. News from Nowhere had a role in them all, providing a focus for solidarity movements, selling Coal not Dole mugs and proudly supporting the "Enemy Within" by collecting for striking miners. They involved themselves in the revival of CND and Women Opposed to the Nuclear Threat (WONT) and generally provided a haven for the disaffected, the disenchanted and the dispossessed. During this time, the bookshop refused to accept Barclays cheques in solidarity with the Anti-Apartheid Movement, and focussed particularly on Ireland. They campaigned around the Hunger Strikes, the Prevention of Terrorism Act, strip searches, the British occupation in general, and supported delegations to the North of Ireland. And although *Liverpool Free Press* had folded, the back rooms of the bookshop were now occupied by a printing firm, Whitechapel Press, and a silkscreen workshop, Sleeping Partners. Badges, posters and post-cards were also stocked: "Nuclear Power No Thanks" in every conceivable language, "Just because you're paranoid it doesn't mean they're not out to get you", "It begins when you sink into his arms and ends with your arms in his sink" — political humour was in evidence everywhere. The most popular poster at the time was a pastiche of the film poster for *Gone With the Wind* featuring a young Ronald Reagan carrying Thatcher, with the words "She promised to follow him to the end of the earth. He promised to organise it", complete with a mushroom cloud in the back-ground. It must be remembered that dissemination of information in the pre-computer age was primarily through print, and books, leaflets, notices and mailings were crucial in every movement for change. Nowadays the bookshop does a weekly email to over six hundred "Friends from Nowhere", but back then it sent out *Little Bird*, a monthly mailing of leaflets, to subscribers, and produced the *Merseyside People's Yellow Pages*.

News from Nowhere had a broadly libertarian, bordering on the anarchist, leaning and was fiercely feminist, which meant it had a lot of criticisms of the "straight" labour movement "left". None more so than Liverpool City Council's Militant period which, while it was admired for its house-building programme and standing up to Thatcher, was nevertheless narrowly white and male-dominated. Militant alienated the Black community and women equally, at a time when Ken Livingstone's GLC and other progressive local governments were recognising and attempting to redress manifestations of oppression and privilege in terms of race, gender, sexuality and disability. Liverpool fell way behind on these issues and the bookshop was definitely on the side of the critical voices. However, the non-aligned and non-sectarian nature of the shop meant it could encompass literature and individual activists and campaigns from every strand of the left and progressive thought. All the major socialist and Marxist newspapers were stocked, notices were displayed for every meeting, demo and action, and alternative viewpoints were always given a voice. This could be another reason for NfN's survival over other narrower-based enterprises.

In the late seventies and early eighties a number of Socialist Bookfairs had been held in London. In 1984 came the First International Feminist Bookfair. NfN responded by holding their own in Liverpool at the Methodist Central Hall in Renshaw Street. It was a gigantic undertaking, involving transporting massive quantities of books to the venue. The daytime Bookfair included authors Barbara Rogers, Maud Sulter and Pat Barker (pre-*Regeneration Trilogy* and relatively unknown at the time), along with workshops, exhibitions and children's storytelling. The evening "Write To Be Free" event featured Indian feminist Madhu Kishwar and anti-apartheid activist Ellen Kuzwayo.

With the bookshop's collective now firmly established as a Workers' Co-operative, its part in the burgeoning co-operative movement on Merseyside became central. A number of new co-ops had started, the local Co-operative Development Agency was encouraging their growth and in 1984 the Women's Independent Cinema House (WITCH) made the film *You'll Never Work Alone* in which NfN featured. Even within this movement the collective pushed the boundaries by rejecting any form of hierarchical structure and asserting that all workers should receive the same wages, on the principle that you work as hard whether you've been there a decade or a day. This remains one of the most revolutionary of the collective's principles.

Another essential aspect was the bookshop's welcome to lesbians and gays and its championing of these liberation struggles. Count has been lost of the number of customers who recall their tentative attempts at coming out and how exhilarating it was to be able to walk into a shop which openly displayed lesbian and gay literature. One friend said recently it scared her to even stand next to the shelf, but she could hardly express how important it was for her. At a time when mainstream bookshops had not yet realised the power of the pink pound, when nightclubs were often the only meeting-places, and when Section 28 was looming on the horizon, NfN was a welcome starting point for young lesbians and gays on their journey to coming out.

In 1989 premises were finally found for an arts centre housing Open Eye, the photographic gallery, and News from Nowhere, in Bold Street, Liverpool's most bohemian street. Bold Street was close to the south, more multicultural, end of the city and a perfect home for the bookshop which was by this time being run by Mandy, Sally Evans, Julie Callaghan and Pauline Lavercombe. Mandy was pregnant, so, to cover her maternity leave, Jill Harris joined the collective. The relief of leaving the Whitechapel building, which, as well as fascists, had rats of the furry variety, constant leaks and floods and nowhere near enough custom to sustain the business, was enormous. 112 Bold Street was a bright, newly-furbished shop on a busy street and the collective set about filling the shop with an even better range of books, a custom-built children's area, enjoying the increased sales and expanding more into author events. The opening of the new building featured local author Moy McCrory with Brookside stars cutting the ribbon. It felt like they had arrived at last, although the relief of being able to get on with running a bookshop without the constant attention of fascist attacks was somewhat tempered by all the old lefties complaining that the atmosphere just wasn't the same. Where was their support of workers' rights — not to work in unhealthy and unsafe workplaces — the NfN staff wondered!

Writers had visited the old shop in Whitechapel, notably Andrea Dworkin and the authors of *Lesbian Nuns: Breaking Silence*, but in Bold Street the bookshop played host to many more rising and risen stars: Sue Johnston, Jeanette Winterson, Tony Benn, Ronan Bennett, Monica Sjöö, Nell McCafferty and Ken Livingstone. In particular, to celebrate the 20th anniversary in 1994, an event was held every month on different aspects of the shop's politics: Eamonn McCann for Ireland, Jackie Kay and Buchi Emecheta for Black writers, Mary Daly for feminism, Lois Keith for disability activism and so on. The only disaster was when the lesbian feminist Sheila Jeffreys walked out as questions began. She had apparently had a hostile grilling all day by the media and seemingly couldn't distinguish between this and a group of feminists wanting to debate her ideas. The meeting continued without her, reflecting NfN's belief that ideas are ultimately more important than any individual.

Meanwhile, the bookshop, being a part of the feminist and lesbian movements, reflected the controversies of the time over issues like racism and lesbian S&M, and many meetings and teach-ins were held to thrash out the viewpoints. NfN also took the lead in providing space for support groups to meet, including survivors of child sexual abuse, the working-class women's writing group and the lesbian mothers group. The collective was heavily involved in the Campaign against Section 28. Later there was to be a critique of the divisiveness of identity politics, but during the 1980s and 90s many issues which were later recognised in mainstream society had their beginnings in small groups finding a home and a voice in places such as radical bookshops, in the same way that feminism had its beginnings in small consciousness-raising groups. Books and politics also converged in the Rushdie Affair. News from Nowhere took the stance of defending Rushdie's right to publish *The Satanic Verses* and supporting him against the fatwa and the burning of the book, having no truck with religious institutions of any kind.

Original and creative events took place such as the Freedom of Sexuality Kissathon in the window one Valentine's Day, and the visits of Mother Xmas to read stories to children. Publicity was given to the Liverpool Dockers' fight, the occupation of the Irish Centre and the Hillsborough Justice Campaign.

At the same time the bookshop was attempting to broaden the diversity of the collective. Judith was the first Black woman to join and she stayed for a number of years, dealing with being the only ethnic minority worker. Not an easy position. A decision was taken to employ *only* Black and Minority Ethnic (BME) women, whenever a vacancy came up, until the collective was at least half non-white. This was never achieved and to this day it remains one of the pressing issues. Liverpool's employment record generally is abysmal as far as BME equality is concerned. News from Nowhere has had limited opportunity to address this imbalance as staff increasingly stay for longer periods. And as the shop workers remain on minimum wage levels this has proven to be a further encumbrance as few BME applicants apply. Although jobs are now advertised to all women, positive discrimination is still applied, all else being equal, and attempts have been made to encourage BME volunteering which can stand people in good stead to apply for future vacancies.

During the 20th birthday celebrations News from Nowhere received a heavy blow. The building fell into the hands of a property company, Frensons, which set about trying to evict the shop. The collective went back into campaigning mode, producing badges saying "Don't Play

Monopoly with Small Businesses", gathering petitions and raising money for a defence campaign. It transpired that the arts organisation the bookshop had been sub-letting from had defaulted on their rent, and although the shop could prove *it* had always paid, this wasn't enough in law to prevent the eviction. Luckily, the health food shop down the road was closing down so an attempt was made to buy the lease. At that point the owner decided he wanted to sell the whole building for £75,000, then an unimaginable cost. Jill had the vision to see what an opportunity this was to put the bookshop on a solid footing, and the collective set about raising the money, plus the same again for refurbishment. Letters were sent out to all and sundry, including every well-known personality with whom the shop had ever been tenuously connected. The first to respond was Victoria Wood! Thousands were raised in donations and interest-free loans from friends and supporters, appalled at the idea of "their" bookshop going under. In fact, whenever there's been the need, News from Nowhere has always put the appeal out and help has been forthcoming. Going public has always been and remains the best strategy. This is one of the reasons so many people identify with News from Nowhere and really feel they have a stake in it — because they have! Amazingly, with the help of a mortgage from the Co-op Bank, loans from ICOF (the co-operative movement's finance arm) and the Andrew Wainwright Trust, the money was raised and a five-storey building at 96 Bold Street, with a 1,200 square-feet ground floor shop was bought in January 1996. The acquisition was arguably the single most important factor in the shop's survival. The ribbon-cutter this time was Alexei Sayle, along with his eighty-year old mum, Molly, herself well-known locally as a passionate revolutionary.

Now the shop could rent out the upper storey to help pay the mortgage. Windows Poetry Project moved in, and soon the Methodist Central Church took over a whole floor and has been a stalwart tenant ever since, running the innovative "Bread Church", an inclusive, diverse and welcoming space. Despite NfN being avowedly atheist in outlook, this has been a positive and mutual relationship. Various other groups have been housed over the years, currently *Nerve*, the arts and culture magazine, Liverpool Pride, and a rented flat at the top. In 2007 the Liverpool Social Centre, known as "Next to Nowhere" was established in the basement, a non-hierarchical space for activism, debates, films, meetings, and a vegan café on Saturdays. The whole building became a hive of activity. In the bookshop the children's area acquired a comfy chair for breastfeeding mothers, together with a toybox, and the kettle reappeared. Instead of Peter the Great, Dr May and Anarchist Bob there were now the various and varied *Big Issue* sellers popping in for a cuppa. Things had come full circle.

The move to being property owners necessitated a change of emphasis in the collective's working practices. Up until then they had rotated most jobs, from cleaning to ordering books and doing the accounts. This was becoming increasingly unwieldy and more continuity was needed as the financial responsibilities expanded. Staff began to specialise. They still all did some cleaning, and shifts on the till, but the big jobs of ordering books, keeping the accounts and managing the building began to fall to different individuals, albeit with decision-making still generally taken in collective meetings.

At the same time, with the ending of the Net Book Agreement in 1997 (by which bookshops could not undercut publishers' retail prices) and the consequent pressures on an independent bookshop that could not compete with the chain bookshops on price, more outlets for selling books had to be sought. News from Nowhere had over the years been supplying books to local schools, specialising in diversity and social issues, supported by the local authority through the Ethnic Minority Achievement Service. Trade came and went with the City

Libraries, as they started to set up exclusive contracts with big supply companies. But one of the enduring relationships was with Liverpool John Moores University. For years sympathetic lecturers had recommended NfN to their students, and this expanded greatly at number 96 as there was now room to stock vast quantities of student texts. Other lecturers realised that NfN was far more efficient than the big chains. Every autumn the influx of students brings much-needed trade and a new generation of young people, many of whom take an interest in other aspects of the bookshop's stock and politics. They are often amazed to discover what a real bookshop looks like as their only idea previously had been the soulless clone-chains. The Liverpool Community College also took to using the bookshop as stockist for their ESOL student texts, which brought in newly arrived immigrants. One of the sections that attracted them once they had acquired their set books was the increasing collection of World Music CDs the shop was selling. This had grown from a few LPs back at Whitechapel to a massive stand of CDs from all over the globe, plus folk, women artists and political music. To this day it seems unlikely that many other records shops have sections for Armenia, Madagascar, Palestine and Galicia.

In 1999 News from Nowhere celebrated its 25th Birthday, with the theme "Now is the Time", to publicise and fund-raise for two campaigns, the Jubilee 2000 Campaign to cancel Third World debt, and the attempt to free Mzwakhe Mbuli, imprisoned South African poet, musician and activist. In the usual tradition of combining books and politics, author events were held with feminist historian Sheila Rowbotham, and with Phil Scraton on the tenth anniversary of the Hillsborough disaster. At the social a local band played South African Township music and there was a Bread and Roses themed refreshment table. Other authors to visit No. 96 included James Kelman, Jean 'Binta' Breeze, Samir Amin and Armistead Maupin — an eclectic bunch.

Meanwhile it was interesting to note the waxing and waning subjects of the bookshop's stock in relation to the politics of the times. During the 1990s books by Marx and on subjects like economics were poor sellers. There was an upsurge of interest in alternative health, self-help therapy and New Age books, and NfN inevitably reflected this. However, unlike some radical bookshops which had turned away from politics to embrace mainstream literature, often to their detriment and eventual demise, NfN never took this route. The assertion of the collective was always that inner and outer change must go hand in hand; both are necessary for the changes we need to see in the world. So while witches and angels crept into the stock, the fiction was always chosen for its depiction of social issues, the children's books always reflected diverse families and multicultural society — even the humour section was purely feminist or satirical... and there were always those masses of left-wing newspapers. Moreover, even when they were very slow to shift, you could always find a vast array of books reflecting international struggles, political theory, anarchism and revolution. And as the anti-roads protests and renewed interest in ecology and environmental issues increased, so did that section. A bookseller is always having to rearrange the shelves, move things up and down to eye-level!

Then came 9/11 and as the politics of the world went into spin, Liverpool's activists once again rejoiced in having a thriving, established radical bookshop to provide them with information, books, notice boards and, above all, an outlet for selling tickets for coaches to demonstrations. As Stop the War's 15th February 2003 demo approached it became obvious that its size would be unprecedented as bookshop staff were unable to get any work done for weeks beforehand with the level of ticket sales for coaches and trains. Suddenly people wanted to find out about U.S. and British imperialism, the history of Afghanistan and Iraq, militarism and its alternatives, the persecution of immigrants, and exactly whose "terrorism" we should be talking about. The anti-roads protests had morphed into critiques of globalisation and capitalism, and concern about climate change and biopiracy and corporate power. News from Nowhere was yet again an invaluable resource; it was never just a question of selling books but more of helping people engage with a subject.

The relationship with other bookshops in Liverpool had often been competitive. It was hard, having pioneered the stocking of lesbian and gay literature in the city, to see a lot of these customers defecting to the chains, which overcame their squeamishness when they realised that the pink pound was a pound after all. But there was always a new subject to pioneer and, as the other radical bookshops had by now all bitten the dust and one by one the city's independents closed their doors, NfN found itself in the strange position of being the major independent in the city. There was now a relatively easy equilibrium as NfN's reputation for efficient and friendly customer service and its Any Book Ordering facility made it a popular destination for general book-lovers as well as die-hard politicos. The shop also responded to Liverpool's intense local pride by championing local history books, which began to draw in more passing trade. In addition, the politics of the shop were no longer seen as quite so scary in a climate of tolerance for sexuality, interest in the environment and championing of diversity issues.

The big change to News from Nowhere's position in the city came in 2004. Joe Sim, a strong supporter of the shop and Professor of Criminology at John Moores University (LJMU), proposed that NfN should be honoured in its thirtieth birthday year by the University. As a result, LJMU bestowed a Lifetime Achievement Award on the bookshop, complete with an oration in the Cathedral on Graduation Day. In addition, through some sympathetic councillors, an invitation was extended to the bookshop and its guests to hold a Civic Reception in the Town Hall. Did it mean News from Nowhere had sold out? As one Chilean revolutionary remarked on the night, "In the old days, we'd have been storming this place." It certainly felt like being brought in from the cold after many a year on the fringes of, if not way outside, respectability. However, Mandy's speech on the night pulled no punches as she reminded the assembled crowd of subversives that the Town Hall and the very streets of the city were built from the blood and toil of Africans during the slave trade, and that racism was the most important issue facing Liverpool today.

The theme for that year's celebration was "We Are All Immigrants", with badges and balloons stating the same, and an interactive map for customers to pinpoint their family origins, which remains in the shop to prove the point.

The latest challenge is the rise and ruthlessness of Amazon, with its aggressive discounting and its attempts to control and dominate the supply of e-books, while paying no UK tax and being heavily criticised for its employment practices. The bookshop has responded by promoting its own website through which people can access a complete list of books in print, browse NfN's own recommended booklists and order online, choosing either mail order or collecting from the shop. In other words, shop with the *real* Amazons. In addition, the collective constantly introduces innovative ideas to enhance the experience of shopping in a real, live bookshop. In-store displays have become more inventive: The Trouble with Religion; No-one is Illegal; the Birds & the Bees (literally about birds and bees); the Big Society Bites Back; and This Land is Our Land: all have featured on the tables. Links with campaigns and community groups have strengthened — many have made use of the shop's high street window to publicise their causes: Mary Seacole House (a project for Black women's mental health), Sahir House (the local HIV/Aids centre), Arabic Arts Festival, Hillsborough Justice Campaign and Football v. Homophobia. International Women's Day, Chinese New Year,

Jewish Book Week, Martin Luther King Day: all are celebrated. And many, many bookstalls are provided for local and national conferences and meetings, including the Women's Aid National Conference, Africa Oye music festival (an outdoor event to which the shop takes a whole marquee full of African CDs) and regional Anarchist Bookfairs, Liverpool Friends of Palestine meetings, local history events and Transition Towns conferences. Many author events which the bookshop covers are associated with two vital partnerships. One is with Writing on the Wall Festival, now in its twelfth year, which every May brings a wide range of cutting-edge writers, hip hop artists and poets to the city and also hosts a series of Rebel Rants by people like Michael Mansfield, Bonnie Greer and Peter Tatchell. The other is the Bluecoat Arts Centre, which until recently held a series of literature events throughout the year, culminating in the Chapter & Verse literature festival. These have provided invaluable opportunities for bookselling as well as rich cultural liaisons, including enabling NfN to fulfil a cherished ambition to bring Gary Younge to Liverpool. It certainly makes the job of bookseller at News from Nowhere very much more than a nine to five one, and self-exploitation and burnout are always in the collective's mind.

Then there are special events such as the Ranters' Corner held on the recent Royal Wedding Day, during which people were invited to step onto a soapbox outside the shop. For two hours the public ranted and raved, sang, recited poetry, got things off their chests and taught each other about issues such as mental health, the attack on benefits for the disabled and the role of the monarchy. It was a brilliant show of people power and just what the bookshop prides itself on — providing a forum for information and debate. Another exciting development in the last few years has been the Bold Street Festival. Bold Street is primarily a street of independent, often quirky shops and cafés, with some great arts projects nearby. NfN has been centrally involved in developing this annual event to celebrate and bring more trade into the street. There have recently been collaborations with more mainstream organisations such as the Liverpool Biennial, Philosophy in the City and the Liverpool Design Festival. The general trend is to say yes to any joint projects so long as NfN is allowed to retain the integrity of its beliefs and politics. One collective member who campaigns against house demolitions has even gone into the lion's den by intervening with property developers on the local "regeneration" committee. And, in 2011 NfN was invited onto the steering group of "Liverpool: City of Radicals", an initiative to commemorate the 1911 Transport Strike.

The collective now comprises Mandy Vere (matriarch), Julie Callaghan (finger on the pulse), Maria Ng (accounts wizard), Cate Simmons (artistic soul), Sara Woodward (building supremo), and Sally, Jill and Rhona (wonderful volunteers).

Bob Dent said, back at the beginning: "To help us create that better world which William Morris envisaged in *News from Nowhere*, we need ideas which counter the prevailing ideologies. Access to alternative, creative, radical ideas, which help us challenge the different power structures of society, is not a sufficient condition for changing the world, but it is a necessary one." Long may News from Nowhere be there to provide that access.

Homeland

Chris Moss

Río Turbio was off the tourist map, just. A small bus had ferried Cecilia, my girlfriend, and I, and a dozen Chilean miners across the Andes at dusk. Forget any ideas about snow-capped peaks and sweeping panoramas; at this latitude the chain is fractured and irregular and the mountain passes low. The miners, who commuted the journey every Sunday and were due on the morning shift the following day, dozed. Outside a cold rain fell, turning to sleet with the dusk.

This was Patagonia in its dreariest expression. I felt marooned, entombed on the bus in a nowhere land. But to the north was the Santa Cruz river valley up which Darwin and FitzRoy had navigated in 1834, sounding inlets and surveying the "informal Empire". They had shared their thoughts on evolutionary theory until some uncharacteristic irresolution on the Captain's part led to their quarrelling. Far away to the northwest was the province of Chubut and another river valley, this one used by the Welsh settlers who had voyaged, in 1865, from Liverpool and found a barren shore; there to establish Y Wladfa — The Colony — they rode across the scrub and followed the Río Chubut till they found valleys fertile enough to grow towns. At around the same time, Butch, Sundance and Etta Place arrived, taking a break from bankrobbing to raise cattle and kick back.

These are the oft-told legends. Many more exist that are local, from a magical barberry that tricks travellers into returning, to a ghost-ship crewed by drowned sailors. Then there were the travellers themselves, who skilfully mythologised their idling and daydreams: Lady Florence Dixie and William Henry Hudson; D'Orbigny and St-Exupéry; Chatwin and Theroux. The last pair did their internships in Patagonia, cribbing others' hard-won research and borrowing their bilingualism to forge a new genre of bookish travelogue.

Patagonia has often played the classical role of eutopia: a good, or even great, place. Its slightly absurd name, coined by Magellan's diarist, has usefully obscure origins: "Patagon" might mean that the Indians observed by Antonio Pigafetta had "big feet", but it probably means their strange guanaco-skin hoods and capes reminded the Vicenza-born diarist of a dog-headed monster of that name, at the time starring in a popular chivalric romance. But Magellan and Pigafetta also saw hogs with navels on their haunches, clawless birds whose hens laid eggs on the backs of their mates and tongueless pelicans; on recording such marvels in his journal, Pigafetta gave birth — so argued Gabriel García Márquez in his Nobel speech — to five hundred years of magic realism.

"Magical" mysteries, half-whispered below deck and in Genoa, Plymouth and St Malo in turn duped conquistadors and chancers into conceiving golden men and gilded cities, fertile planes and fecund women, extant dinosaurs and extinct tribes. This last came true. Layer upon layer of story settled on the wastes and even now, should you park your car and wander off into the near-desert, the half-hearted Patagonian desert, you are wading through myth, fable, rumour, lie. A man in Río Gallegos once told me Eva Braun had joined the one-way package tours to Argentina granted to all good Nazis by her namesake, Señora Perón. Everyone and anyone can be imagined coming to Patagonia.

During the Cold War years, the region's paradoxical combination of *tabula rasa* and hectic mythopoeia may have aided its entry into the exclusive club of nuclear-free zones. No one on either side, the doom-mongers agreed, would bother to direct an ICBM at the arse-end of South America's arse-end: *el culo del mundo*, as the locals say. The land was envisioned as refuge and retreat, projector screen and Eden. Escapees from the targetted countries of the West had an invitation to relocate far, far away from all the geopoliticking. Eutopia blurred with utopia – nowhere was paradise, and this time it came in the shape of a huge, roofless, wind-blasted bunker.

No one took up the offer.

In Río Turbio's one crappy hotel there was one option for the evening meal: lentil and tripe stew. It was difficult to connect this meagre offering with abundant Argentina. Where were the pornographic steaks, *las pastas de mamá* and the sickly-sweet pastries of the northern pampas towns? Weren't there trout and salmon in the mountain streams? Or at least some mutton from the steppe to help down with a hefty malbec?

But Río Turbio was pinched, shrivelled, inchoate. It felt like a place that couldn't be bothered to exist. Cecilia and I spooned our greasy lentils and vaguely grumbled, as couples on holiday will, until it was nearly bedtime. After an attempt at a night-stroll, we hit our twin sacks — I can't remember if we made love or even kissed goodnight. I, at least, was mellow with boredom and a serene kind of depression. Whatever Río Turbio lacked, it seemed to promise something too, and I slept deeply, untroubled by legends.

In the morning, after a breakfast of Nescafé and stale white bread, I was anxious to walk, to get up on higher ground and take a view. The rain had stopped, so we wrapped up and set off into the town.

Before I was able to see Río Turbio, I felt it. I sensed something that was entirely new to me. Until arriving in the town, we'd been on a typical backpacker journey from Buenos Aires, down to Argentina's lake district, across the border to voyage by ship down through the Chilean fjords to wind up at a walkable cluster of granite mountains inside a national park. We'd met people along the way — people from all nations and all similar to us — and slept in tents and hostels, taken photographs and done a lot of sitting around waiting for transport. Our travelling had been a mixture of wide-eyed superficiality, insincere socialising and mild fatigue, My observational faculties had been overworked, and my mind and heart were in sleep mode.

But in Río Turbio I experienced a familiarity that wasn't borne of any routine or mental dullness. We had wandered out to the edge of town (or perhaps the edge of town had wandered in) and found ourselves standing before a railway siding. As an old steam-powered engine was being readied to cross the southern Patagonian steppe to the port at Río Gallegos, with loud coughs and hisses, an aromatic cloud of coal, steam and oil — an eye-watering concoction — drifted over on the breeze. Mental schemata were fuelled, then fired. Born in 1966, I'm a post-steam child, but I knew the smell.

We walked slowly away, passing through a low-slung residential quarter. Down the grey streets, small groups of miners — among them probably some of the sleepers from the bus — trudged to work. They looked resigned, stoical, grounded. The opposite of travellers.

After cursorily checking the "centre", such as it was in this half-born town, we decided Río Turbio offered little in the way of built diversion and headed out towards a slope on another periphery. Not a hill, but a mere brow, rather like a grassed-over slag heap. There was a narrow, irregular pathway, also oddly familiar, which had the appearance of something the locals had created through repeated use rather than design and which led outwards and upward. We were not in hiking territory. There were no sheep around to tread their own dirt tracks. This was ordinary suburban near-wasteland, mainly ruderal with scraps of rubbish tossed here by the polar wind. The grassland that survived was yellow, the soil beneath a dull brown colour, as if dried out. With the cloud cover above complete, there was no kind, active light falling on the landscape at all. You had the feeling brilliance was being drained out of nature. We cast no shadows. Were the pits below leaching out the goodness? Had decades of industry poisoned the land?

The train left town with a huff and a puff and small black clouds rose into the sky. A stray dog joined us for the slow walk along the path, which ascended gradually until, finally, Río Turbio lay before us in a wide untidy valley.

In no real sense had I arrived anywhere at that moment, yet I felt the simplest and deepest of pleasures after only a tiny pause. It suddenly struck me what Río Turbio was for me.

I had — it seemed — stumbled upon a facsimile of my place of birth in South Lancashire. The sights, sounds, smells and other sensory correlatives of Río Turbio were precisely, or sufficiently precisely, those of Burtonwood, my village, and its nearest — extinct, Thatcher-slain — collieries: Bold, Parkside, Sutton Manor. My dad mined at the middle one, driving some mysterious machine he never properly explained. This town, if anything, if it could be bothered to be anything, was like a pared-down version of St Helens, a risible idea since the original is hardly overwrought.

I'm no dreamer. I have no astral ambitions and I hadn't opened a cosmic portal. I'd merely chanced upon a form of my homeland — the one where I was born and raised and fed and bedded till the age of 18 — and with it my infancy, my family, my school days, my puberty and early trials, all began to course through my mind even as the landscape lay still and seeming-dead. And I'd found it in a far-off place. I was in the contrary hemisphere, but due to an accidental configuration of meteorology, geology, social history — and maybe mood, the towns and mine — I was inhabiting a familiar space. I'd found, in Río Turbio, home, and all the longing for home that is innate to us welled up in me. The boredom that calmed me was archetypal, definitive — welling not up but deep down to some endless school holiday that now stretches off into southern Patagonia.

2011: Río Turbio is now on the tourist map, just. People come to play at being *gaucho* for a day or to see a sculpture park of wooden goblins. No doubt boredom is at a premium, and tripe too, But I doubt even the keenest gentrifiers and regenerators could quite tear that Lancastrian pneuma from its soul.

I'm not sure what year we went to Patagonia. 1993? Or was it '94? I cannot recall where we went afterwards on that long, exploratory holiday. If Río Turbio has stayed with me like the clouds for Brecht's Baal in *Remembering Marie A*, it has to do with the unsaleable, the unpackageable aspects of modern travel — the cheap-rate sublime we need: sweet sorrow, the spirit of pointlessness, profound yet gentle boredom.

I've since wondered — having found myself working as a travel writer — whether travel isn't actually always about a search for home. Perhaps Río Turbio was the ultimate arrival for me: the sameness of home, but intangible and specious and mysterious because it wasn't that at all, but an illusion that I could be in two places at once, rooted and free, a child and a man, entranced by dull ordinariness and thus on the edge of my own small myth.

Marge Piercy's Non-Utopia in *Woman on the Edge of Time*

Deirdre O'Byrne

'Rocket ships, skyscrapers into the stratosphere, an underground mole world miles deep, glass domes over everything? She was reluctant to see this world.' That's what Harlem inhabitant Connie Ramos thought when she travelled telepathically to Mattapoisett 2137, and it echoed my own thoughts before first reading Marge Piercy's *Woman on the Edge of Time.* I hadn't been a fan of *Star Trek*, had never seen *Star Wars*, and assumed I'd be equally unmoved by a novel involving time-travel. I cannot defend this prejudice: I happily amble backwards into the worlds of Dickens and Austen, and sideways with any number of novelists, but I have travel sickness at the thought of a readerly propulsion into the twenty-second century. 'What did I expect from the future ... Pink skies? Robots on the march? Transistorised people?' I wasn't sure, but I was fairly certain I wouldn't like it.

But I like a challenge, so I settled down to read it and was immediately unsettled. The opening scene is graphically violent, as Connie, a second-generation Mexican woman existing on welfare in a 1970s tenement, is attacked by Geraldo, her niece Dolly's pimp. Connie hits him in turn as he tries to force an abortion on Dolly, and ends up in a mental hospital, as the authorities take the word of the well-dressed pimp over that of a shabby woman with a past history of mental illness. Signed in by her brother Luis, Connie is thrown into seclusion, heavily drugged, in 'a hall with no door and no windows' with 'four filthy walls'. So, yes, it turns out that this is a novel about space, but not in the way I'd expected; when we get a chance to temporarily escape from Connie's present grim reality into the future with Luciente, it's a relief to find ourselves in a village where everyone has their own living space, and the salt-tanged air is filled with laughter and birdsong. Release from incarceration in Rockover in Connie's world would take her back to a life of loneliness and poverty in a tenement in El Barrio, Spanish Harlem, to a life which has been a 'dark journey' so far. Luciente's Mattapoisett represents the kind of freedom she has never experienced and can barely imagine, where women have 'an air of brisk unselfconscious authority Connie associated with men'. Luciente, whose name means 'shining, brilliant, full of light', is Connie's guide to the future world, but her body language at first leads Connie to perceive her as male. This is one of the many instances in which the novel shows how traditional femininity in the present hampers women, whereas in the future they develop in a more androgynous environment.

This contrast is key to Piercy's technique throughout the novel: the writer confronts us with a present which is obviously flawed, with restrictions which damage the characters we meet. Whether inside or outside an institution, people are shown to be trapped in unhappy lives. Connie, Dolly and Luis's third wife Adele resort to drugs at times of crisis. Many of the men in the present are physically violent, like Connie's father and her husband Eddie, or verbally cruel, like Luis. Inside the mental hospital, we encounter characters who appear to be social misfits, but it's the rigid categories into which people are expected to fit that are the problem, not the patients' refusal or inability to conform. As Luciente says to Connie, 'in truth you don't seem mad to me.' Rebellious Alice, Sybil the self-defined witch, and homosexual Skip are regarded as 'monsters' but, especially in contrast to the hospital staff, appear comparatively sane.

Piercy makes it clear that the real-time present of the novel is the same as her time of writing by referring to 1976 in chapter fifteen. This 1970s society, which condemns people for following their natural inclinations, is juxtaposed with a future in which some of the present's problems have been solved. Many of the solutions involve a change of attitude. For instance, the stigma around mental illness no longer exists: in Mattapoisett, Luciente explains, they do not use 'sick' and 'mad' interchangeably. Piercy does not suggest that madness can be eradicated from human experience, and we hear of episodes in which people retreat to heal themselves or be healed, but, as in Doris Lessing's *The Golden Notebook*, there is a creative side to breakdown. Luciente declares herself too 'flat-footed and earthen' to go mad, whereas healer Diana and artist Jackrabbit 'go down' into themselves from time to time and emerge with renewed energies. In the cases we observe in Rockover, by contrast, time spent in a mental institution is neither creative nor restorative: 'The mental hospital had always seemed like a bad joke; nothing got healed in here.' Skip's parents, unwilling to accept his homosexuality, send him for treatment at the age of thirteen 'to be fixed'; he undergoes various programmes including shock therapy, leading him to repeatedly attempt suicide until he succeeds. In the future, we meet Jackrabbit, Skip's futuristic doppel-gänger, who enjoys sexual freedom and is admired and loved rather than rejected. Similarly, Sybil the witch has a 2137 counterpart in Diana the healer, who has high social status and a band of admirers. Piercy tries to show what a society might look like when people's characteris-tics and gifts are cherished rather than deplored or ignored. Luciente compliments Connie on her telepathic abilities: 'You're an extraordinary top catcher. In our culture you would be much admired, which I take it isn't true in this one?' Their telepathic abilities complement each other as Luciente acts as 'sender' to Connie's 'catcher'.

On first sight, Connie perceives Mattapoisett society as being back in 'the dark ages', as the village reminds her of her peasant uncle Tío Manuel's, with its vegetable plots and goats. In this aspect, Piercy's novel is an early example of eco-feminism — the exploitation of women, as in the prostitution of Dolly, is paralleled by mistreatment of the earth. The book seems prescient too, in its championing of sustainable farming, composting, natural fertiliser and recycling. Piercy has drawn on many so-called primitive societies in her construction of the future, for example, teenagers go through an initiation ceremony, spending a week alone in the wilderness as transition into adulthood. She also draws on influential theories of the twentieth century. As Virginia Woolf recommends in *A Room of One's Own*, each adult has their own separate living area. Luciente is shocked at the idea of living 'piled together' and explains that 'you have space of your own. How could one live otherwise? How meditate, think, compose songs, sleep, study?' This is clearly the opinion of a writer. Piercy's Jewish background surfaces in the many similarities between the ideals of Mattapoisett and the original kibbutzim, which aimed for collective, collaborative societies with sexual equality, communal child-rearing and socialist values. Kibbutzim in the early days were agrarian, and were kept deliberately small, echoing Luciente's declaration that 'we don't have *big* cities — they didn't work'.

However, technology is an important part of Piercy's fictional future. Repetitive jobs are automated, and Luciente works on genetic modification of plants. Homes have solar panels and transport is in 'floaters', a type of hovercraft. Piercy has also worked on the potential sexism inherent in language and in family structures, major concerns of the women's movement in the 1970s. The difficulties that Connie experiences in distinguishing some people's gender is exacerbated by the elision of gendered pronouns, to be replaced by the androgynous 'per'. Sexual couplings are free from prejudice and legal or religious bindings, whether one is drawn to one's own sex or another. Each child has three parents, of either sex, who co-mother it. As Piercy herself comments, three parents allows for eight-hour shifts, which gives everyone a reasonable chance of getting some rest. Most radical of all is the future concept of birth. The reproductive system has moved out of the body and into the brooder: a 'space that looked more like a big aquarium than a lab', where embryos grow into babies. Connie is disgusted by this 'baby factory', but Luciente explains that 'It was part of women's long revolution... Finally there was one thing which we had to give up too... the power to give birth. Cause as long as we were biologically enchained, we'd never be equal.' This reasoning is similar to that put forward by Shulamith Firestone in *The Dialectic of Sex* (1970), in which she argues that women's childbearing abilities are responsible for biological determinism. Connie is initially resistant to what she regards as 'canned' babies, but comes to the realisation that her daughter, in a society like Mattapoisett, would have had a chance to 'grow up much better and stronger and smarter than I'. In 2012, we can see that Piercy's world now seems more achievable. The first test-tube baby was born in 1978, two years after *Woman on the Edge of Time* was published. Aarathi Prasad's book, *Like a Virgin: How Science is Redesigning the Rules of Sex*, predicts that we'll see artificial wombs within forty years, if we overcome barriers of regulation and ethics alongside the technology.

Piercy herself does not see her created future as Utopian. In a 1977 interview, she says: 'There's almost nothing there except the brooder not accessible now. So it's hardly a utopia; it is very intentionally not a utopia because it's not strikingly new. The ideas are the ideas basically of the women's movement.'[1] Time-travel works in both directions in this book, as Piercy uses her imaginary future society to interrogate the present and the past. In flashbacks throughout the novel, we learn more about Connie, a second-generation Mexican who's determined to escape the fate of her mother. Aged fifteen, she declares: 'I won't grow up like you Mamá! To suffer and serve. Never to live my own life! I won't!' Mariana's response, 'You'll do what women do,' suggests a fatalism about her gendered destiny. However, what the novel shows is that Connie's inability to move herself out of poverty is not just due to the fact that she's female. Her brother Luis is wealthy, but he has become so at a cost, shedding wives and humanity as he does so, changing from Connie's beloved sibling to a bully she barely recognises. Connie's gender is shown to be only one factor in her failing to achieve her ambitions, as she falls pregnant in college and has to abandon her studies. There are other issues that are class- and race-related. When Connie's beloved partner Claud dies in prison because he volunteers for a drugs experiment, she collapses into a haze of drunken grief in which she loses her temper and hits her daughter Angelina, who is taken into care and subsequently adopted. What Piercy makes clear is that Connie's anger is caused as much by poverty as by grief: Angelina had ruined her only pair of shoes, which her mother could not afford to replace. Her rage against her daughter is also shown to be a product of self-loathing: 'to love you must love yourself... especially to love a daughter you see as yourself reborn', and Connie felt it was a 'crime to be born poor as it was a crime to be born brown'. The inference is that if Connie had been white and well-off, the authorities would not have been so quick to take her child from her, but she was powerless.

'Most people hit kids. But if you were on welfare and on probation and the whole social-pigeon-holing establishment had the right to trek regularly through your kitchen looking in the closets and under the bed, counting the bedbugs and your shoes, you had better not hit your kid once.'

Connie is hospitalised for eight months with a breakdown after Claud's death, and agrees to the adoption without fully understanding what she is doing. When she hits Geraldo, he and the authorities draw on Connie's previous record, which presents her 'history of child abuse' and mental illness, so she is incarcerated again.

In between these flashbacks into Connie's miserable past and present, we travel with her to Mattapoisett, for lessons in what an alternate life could be like. Each visit brings a new revelation: she observes how relationships work, enjoys a celebration, and witnesses a death. Luciente becomes the avatar of Piercy, showing us how society could function if we chose, and Connie becomes our mouthpiece, voicing questions and objections. In effect, Piercy's novel is her way of 'sending' a message to us, hoping we like Connie will choose to be 'catchers' and realise that we need to modify our behaviours to create the society we want. To drive the point home, Connie accidentally arrives in chapter fifteen in a dystopian world. She meets Gildina, a silicone-enhanced 'cartoon of femininity', who occupies a windowless apartment in a New York of the future, in which poor people function as 'walking organ banks' for 'richies'. She is on short-term sexual contract to a man called Cash, paralleling Dolly's involvement with a series of pimps. She eats processed food, takes drugs, and relies on technology for entertainment, a life which she depicts as privileged in comparison to others, but which mirrors many of the circumstances of life in Rockover, the mental hospital.

Connie thinks, 'This could not exist simultaneously with Mattapoisett. Could not.' As Luciente tries to explain to her: 'We are only one possible future... Alternate universes exist. Probabilities clash and possibilities wink out forever.' This is the basic message of the novel, that we need to actively make positive choices. Piercy, a long-time activist, strives to politicise her readers, as Connie's new friends encourage her to recognise her potential for resistance: 'There's always something you can deny your oppressor, if only your allegiance. Your belief. Your co-oping.' Luciente refers to Connie's life in 1976 as 'the Age of Greed and Waste', and 'fat, wasteful, thing-filled times', contrasting it with their careful husbanding of resources in Mattapoisett, and heralding the urge for conservation that is now common ecological discourse.

There are several other features of Piercy's Mattapoisett which have become part of our twenty-first-century lives. The 'kenner', a computerised 'memory annex' used to contact people and to access information, which Luciente wears on her wrist, is similar to a smartphone. Luciente confesses that she feels 'naked without my kenner. It's part of my body. I only take it off to couple or to sleep... For some it's only convenience. For others part of their psyche', which reflects many of our contemporaries' attitude to their iPhone. For a book that emerged before we became dependent on mobile communication gadgetry, this is an extraordinary feat of foresight on Piercy's part. There's one amusing example of a neologism in the book, when Jackrabbit is discussing his intention to go on active defence, a sort of voluntary national service. He explains to Connie that he is going out of a sense of social duty, and tells her, 'I don't twitter to go,' meaning that he's not all that keen. Nowadays, a contemporary Jackrabbit would undoubtedly express his reluctance online in 140 characters.

Piercy's insistence that her Mattapoisett is not a Utopia because it is possible echoes Margaret Atwood's assertions about her own novels *A Handmaid's Tale* and *Oryx and Crake*, that they are not science fiction but rather speculative fiction, because they depict events that have, or could, actually come about. It is predictable that Atwood and Piercy have produced insightful reviews of each other's work. Writing about the Mattapoisett sequences in *Woman on the Edge of Time*, Atwood commented: 'Some reviewers treated this part of the book as a regrettable daydream or even a hallucination caused by Connie's madness. Such an interpretation undercuts the entire book.'[2] It's an interpretation which is undermined by the determined realism of the opening chapter, in which Dolly finds that the chair Luciente has vacated is still warm. Just after an initial meeting, Connie detects on her own arm traces of

Luciente's characteristic smell, which comes from the chemical she works with. In Connie, whose viewpoint we share throughout the book, Piercy presents a consistent and understandable consciousness. Luciente, a character represented as equally consistent, repeatedly tells Connie that she is not hallucinating.

What appears in the narrative as unrealistic is the future Connie fleetingly imagines when she hears that her niece is pregnant: 'Like figures of paper, like a manger scene of pasteboard figures, a fantasy... she and Dolly and Dolly's children would live together. She would have a family again, finally.' This book is Piercy's call to arms, a warning and a manifesto. Luciente tells Connie, 'I can't interfere in the past... but I can give you advice.' She calls Connie 'my rose', and given that she lives in Spanish Harlem, I am reminded of the song:

> There is a rose in Spanish Harlem...
> It's growing in the street
> right up through the concrete
> But sweet and soft and dreamin'.[3]

The novel puts the onus on us readers to enable women like Connie to grow 'up through the concrete', to contemplate a different way of being, a society with shorter work hours, a chance to choose to work at interesting tasks, and life-long learning. I'd go for that.

References

[1] Marge Piercy, *Parti-Colored Blocks for a Quilt*, University of Michigan Press, 1982

[2] Margaret Atwood, *Second Words: Selected Critical Prose*, Beacon, 1984

[3] 'Spanish Harlem', recorded by Ben E. King 1961. Words and music by Jerry Lieber and Phil Spector

Further Reading

Marge Piercy, *Woman on the Edge of Time*, Knopf (USA), 1976, Women's Press (UK), 1979

Aarathi Prasad, *Like a Virgin: How Science is Redesigning the Rules of Sex*, Oneworld, 2012

Kerstin W. Shands, *The Repair of the World: The Novels of Marge Piercy*, Greenwood, 1994

Catching a Bus to Paradise

Dennis Hardy

From the window of my temporary home in central Adelaide I am constantly bemused to see a bus departing regularly for Paradise. Surely, I ponder, the Promised Land is not so easily reached. After all, the record of travellers in search of utopia is littered with tales of hardship, despair and ultimate failure. And yet every fifteen minutes, passengers climb aboard a yellow bus and one can only assume they achieve their destination. There must be a catch.

In the early sixteenth century, Thomas More described the perfect place that was to lend its name to the whole utopian genre — even though it was only the name that was new, as utopian ideas had already existed for as long as people dreamt of a better life. More located his make-believe world on a remote island that would be hard if not impossible for outsiders to find. In an age of exploration, others, too, used this ploy, favouring distant locations for their place of perfection, beyond the corrupting influence of ordinary mortals. But why stop at an island when one can look, instead, to a place in the clouds, beneath the surface of the sea, or perhaps a lost valley? And this is exactly the kind of venue that different utopians have described.

In ancient Greece, Plato turned to the skies to emphasize the fantasy of the concept, leading his world-weary travellers from Athens to Cloudcuckooland where, in consort with the birds, there was heady talk of a new society. Also with ancient roots, there is the alluring legend of Atlantis, an island idyll that eventually disappeared into the murky depths of the ocean. Utopias are often rooted in real events and this particular myth may well have been based on the sudden demise of the Minoan civilisation in Crete, reputedly the result of a volcanic eruption on the neighbouring island of Santorini. Much later, and even with the world fully explored, the intrepid utopian can still find a hidden corner where the imagination can enjoy free rein. This is what James Hilton did after the Second World War with his discovery of the exotic land of Shangri-La, a beautiful valley where the horrors of earthly conflict were left far behind. There is always room for another utopia.

Of course, no matter where they are, all utopias by their very nature are not what they seem; like a mirage in the desert they habitually fade as one nears them. Alas, as the ambiguity of the term reveals, what is a good place (*eu*-topia) is also no place (*u-topia*). The evidence of impossibility is stark but, as if in defiance of the obvious, it seems that we never choose to read the runes. That is why, every bit as gullible as the many idealists who have earlier set forth on a similar quest, I ignored utopian history and patiently joined a short queue for the bus to Paradise. I handed over my two dollars for a single journey (cautiously turning down the offer of a return ticket as, if it lived up to expectations, I might not, of course, wish to come back) and settled in my seat on my way to this brave new world. But then, no sooner had the bus pulled away than doubts set in.

As the salutary tale of the wooden doll, Pinocchio, came to mind, I thought that even a child would know this must be a fool's errand. Pinocchio, one recalls, was a gullible puppet too easily led to a land of wonderment, only to find to his cost that there was no such place at all. Was there not, too, a hint of this in the story of Dorothy, the girl from Kansas, and her new-found friends who ventured forth along the yellow-brick road, naïvely believing that all their wishes were soon to be fulfilled? Fortified by the prospect of what lay ahead, they overcame various obstacles along the way, emerging each time with right on their side. But the reality of the Emerald City was not as expected and the legendary

Wizard of Oz proved to be no more than a fraud. Confronted with the truth, the lesson of Mid-Western morality was that we should all be thankful for what we have and not be driven to strive for the impossible. Many a priest from the pulpit has delivered the same message. Food for thought as the bus bounced along and Paradise came closer.

Traffic problems are surprisingly few in Adelaide and we made our way without interruption along the wide streets and across a broad belt of parkland that surrounds what is known, for obvious reasons, as 'the square mile'. In the year before Queen Victoria came to the throne, one of her country's loyal servants, Colonel William Light, who had already distinguished himself on the battlefield in the Napoleonic Wars, was asked to design a capital for the newly acquired colony of South Australia. With the title of Surveyor-General, Light turned his back on a more obvious coastal setting, in favour of an inland site with a natural water supply. Good thinking, given the propensity to drought for which the region is renowned ('the driest State in the driest continent'). His plan for the city was simple enough — a regular grid of streets, a mile long on all sides, fringed by indigenous parkland. This is still the core of what is now a metropolis and the broad thoroughfares, wide enough to turn a bullock cart, have served well in response to the demands of modern transport. With an additional flourish, the Surveyor-General laid out a second area of streets and parkland, above the flood plain of the life-giving River Torrens, to create North Adelaide.

Many would say that it was time enough to leave the bus then and there, while still within Light's original township. Adelaide makes no claim to be utopia but it has for long won plaudits as an unusually well-planned and 'liveable' city. In the nineteenth century, the Victorian inventor of the garden city, Ebenezer Howard, acknowledged the pioneering work of the founders of South Australia, who had ahead of their time provided such a convincing demonstration of good planning. Given this recognition, it was fitting that a garden city evangelist, Charles Reade, should in 1916 become the State's first town planner. By then, Adelaide's growth had already taken it beyond the parklands onto land that was cheaper, but Reade wanted to ensure that future development was every bit as good as Light's original settlement. Rather than see it spread at random, he tried to guide new housing into model garden suburbs with an outer swathe of parklands. Even though the burgeoning city was not so easily tamed — and the original development is now no more than the core of a linear metropolis that snakes over some ninety kilometres from north to south — the South Australian capital is often regarded as one of the world's most attractive cities. Fringed along its entire length by the wooded Adelaide Hills and with the ocean no more than a tram ride away, it enjoys a boldly defined setting where nature is never far away. With world-famous wine-growing areas to both north and south, there are times when it might almost be heaven on earth.

So why go in search of somewhere better? Why not be satisfied with what we have already? Alas, utopians have been asked this many times before and always the answer comes in the form of another question: how can we be sure that true perfection cannot be found just over the horizon? How do we know that the best is not yet be found? Although I discover from a fellow passenger that Paradise is no more than a twenty-minute journey, for me it might just as well be over the rainbow, and so I continue to live in hope.

Past the Botanic Gardens and the National Wine Centre goes the bus. It is a Sunday and outside the showcase of the nation's finest vineyards there are tables under the trees, where diners in the mid-afternoon are laughing over glasses of wine. Adelaide is reputed to have more restaurants per capita than any other Australian city and a good time is had by many. A common theme in early utopias was of a land of plenty, where normally famished and downtrodden peasants sat around tables groaning with food, served by priests and princes in a dramatic reversal of roles. After a history of human toil, could it be that the utopian dream of a state of leisure and abundance has finally been realised? Hungry Jack's and KFC, McDonald's and Subway are dotted along the highways, dispensing buckets of food as if it were a mediaeval feast day. Arms reach out from cars as drive-in facilities make it even easier to take one's fill. Shades of the peasant utopia, the Land of Cockaygne, where geese roasted on the spit cried out 'Geese, all hot, all hot!' and larks flew straight into a hungry person's mouth.

But enough of daydreaming. The 'bendy bus' has left the road to join a dedicated track, known as the O-Bahn, gathering speed on its journey to Paradise. Some years ago the misguided city planners ripped up most of the tramways and have since spent inordinate amounts of time and money trying to put them back. Separated from highway traffic with its own track, the O-Bahn offers one kind of solution. Many utopians are anti-urban — preferring to think of the world in a natural state — but there are others who put their faith in new technologies, extolling the virtues of the modern city. H.G. Wells marvelled at the potential of rapid communications, as did the Italian Futurists, but it was Le Corbusier and his Modernist friends who set the mould for the twentieth century. In a radical break with the past, Le Corbusier raised his buildings to the sky, bringing light and air to people who had traditionally lived in dingy surroundings. The ground was then released for a hierarchy of road and rail routes, and even an airstrip located perilously between tower blocks. Something as tame as the O-Bahn would barely have aroused his interest, but it is at least a variation on the same theme. Speed and mass movement were integral to this concept of a brave new world.

Distant thoughts are jolted when suddenly the bus leaves its track and comes to a halt in Paradise. Should one kiss the ground like the Pope when he arrives in a new land? Instead, I ask a bemused couple where I can find the centre of this heavenly place. But there is no centre, they say, 'this is a suburb'. If I want shops I need to get back on the bus and go on to Modbury. But it is not shops that I want and so I ask, instead, in which direction I should walk to Paradise. 'Over there', they say, 'until you reach the reservoir'. The reservoir, I later discover, was built in 1860 as the first of its kind to supply fresh water to Adelaide.

So Paradise is a suburb. For some the very idea of this form of urban growth is anathema but suburbs also have their fervent advocates. Frank Lloyd Wright, the American architect, portrayed his own version of utopia in the 1930s with homes in large plots spread across the vast landscape of the Mid-West. Never mind what traditional urbanists and Modernists were thinking at the time (both groups much preferring compact cities), this is what he believed people actually wanted. In what Wright termed Broadacre City, the car would be king, but gas was cheap then and it was long before sustainability had come onto the agenda.

Closer to home and later in the century, Hugh Stretton, an Adelaide historian with a strong social agenda, wrote a fascinating book called *Ideas for Australian Cities*. In this he defended the suburb against its metropolitan critics, arguing that life can be just as interesting and diverse on a quarter-acre plot as in a city tenement or a country town. If people want to lead dreary lives they will do so wherever they are. Especially as suburbs mature, life behind the corrugated fences that Australian home-owners love can be just as quirky and non-conformist as anywhere else, and at least there is space to pursue one's interests.

Taking the first steps into Paradise, on a sunny autumn afternoon, it was hard not to like the suburb. It is said that it got its enviable name from the first settlers in the district, an English family called Ind, who planted orchards close to the nearby River Torrens and marvelled at the quality and abundance of their harvests. This must be 'truly paradise' they said. There are few signs now of the early market gardens and, at first sight, Paradise is no more than a conventional suburb. New Urbanists might rail against the sterility of this kind of place and claim that its layout is unsustainable but the scene on a sunny afternoon was little short of idyllic. Single-storey houses set in decent-sized plots, the gardens filled with late-flowering bougainvillea, date palms rising above the roofline and trees laden with an early crop of oranges, with the verdant backcloth of the Adelaide Hills. Little *culs de sac* with names like Peaceful Court and Tranquil Court completed the picture. It seemed pretty good to me. And all of this just a twenty-minute commute by public transport into the city.

Even the absence of commerce, no doubt a bane to the residents who just want to pop out for a carton of milk, has its appeal. After all, utopians can often be quite puritanical and it was no coincidence that Ebenezer Howard reserved the centre of his garden city for civic buildings rather than shops, and that the garden city pioneers were averse to sites for drinking establishments. The first garden city pubs sold cocoa and lemonade. As if to make the point that Mammon has no place here, the largest building is the Paradise Community Church. Could there be a better name for a place of worship? But even heaven, it seems, now has a website, so I search on www.paradisecommunitychurch.com to find that this is, indeed, a hotbed for evangelism. An auditorium that can seat 3000 believers is a sign of its local following, with its leaders, Pastors Ashley and Jane, also reaching out to a much wider congregation across the nation through television and online coverage. Certainly, it would seem, the voice of the Lord can be heard in Paradise.

Back through the quiet streets I wander, until the peace is broken by the sound of a domestic argument in one of the yards. Although not wanting to intrude, I cannot help but see an elderly Greek woman berating her seemingly defenceless husband in her mother tongue. Am I to interpret this in a positive way as a sign of the cosmopolitan population in Paradise, the various ethnic groups living side by side, or instead as evidence that even in a place like this discord cannot be excluded? How many utopian schemes have been designed in fine detail, only to be undermined by human frailties? When Adam and Eve were banished from the Garden of Eden, we should have learnt the enduring lesson but, of course, we prefer to ignore it. Utopia could be perfect, one might conclude, if it were not for people. So why, in spite of everything, do we persist in putting our faith in a world that we know is unattainable? Yet more to think about as I make my way back to the bus for the return trip to the city.

Paradise is soon behind me and there is time to reflect on whether it was a wasted journey, another lost quest in the history of the human search for utopia. No, it was certainly not wasted. Not only was it a pleasant experience in itself but, filled with the hope of perfection, there are always revealing questions to be answered. Is one place better than another, and why? In practical terms, how close to perfection can we ordinary mortals get? Is there any point in creating a perfect physical space if the lives of its residents remain rooted in a competitive, unjust world? What can utopia tell us about the society in which we live? Should one even set out on the road to utopia if one knows that the destination will always be beyond reach? In essence, utopia is a frame of mind, questioning what we might otherwise take for granted and encouraging thoughts of how to make things better. And who would gainsay that?

There is barely time enough to pursue these thoughts before the bus comes to a halt in the centre of Adelaide. Ahead of me on the pavement is a family returning from the zoo, the children clutching mementoes and chattering excitedly. A group of young men are gathered outside a pizza kitchen, all of them intent on their mobiles while talking. Parrots dart between the trees, easily visible now that the leaves are falling. The afternoon draws to a close and the sky is transformed by a vivid sunset that casts a warm glow over the whole city. This is real life, not utopia. Or is it utopia and not real life? Past generations would probably say it is, a world of ease and plenty beyond their own wildest hopes; and so would a majority of the world's population now, steeped in poverty and conflict, for whom this is seemingly an impossible dream. Utopia is a relative concept. Adelaide might not tick all the boxes, but in the scheme of things a twenty-minute bus ride can take one at least half-way to Paradise. Or, in the words of a Phil Collins lyric:

Oh
Think twice
'Cause it's another day
For you and me
In paradise.

in the shadow of chimneys

Paul Summers

we danced our infant summers
in the shadow of chimneys
each episode a symphony
of bar-code light, clinging
like hockle to a blackleg's face
painted like legend on
the same bruising cobbles
that shoeless bairns had hopped
& scotched upon in onetimewhen

we left our mark on the chapel wall
unfinished hearts & *shaz 4 paul*
in dripping gloss we'd filched from dad
our tributes daubed in darker times
with fuck the state & *mick's a scab*

we stalked the kids at number 12
like golding's boys with savage blood
with skewer spears of penknived birch
for crimes of having gardens

we played our clammy sex-games
on the elderberried wasteground
fingering our hairless forms
perfecting all our rendezvous
until the call for dinner came

we engineered a world of foes
of japs & huns, arapahos
but fought our wars of sticks & stones
for the tenderness of nurses

we carved ourselves a lost boy's world
entrenched ourselves in no-man's land
set vietcong traps against the old
we dug until our fingers bled

we danced our infant summers
in the shadow of chimneys
each episode a symphony
of bar-code light, clinging
like hockle to a blackleg's face

Keep It In The Family

Pippa Hennessy

Me, seven years old, standing in the hall, crying,
Dad on all fours, rummaging in the under-stairs cupboard.
A heart-wrenching scream from me, "But that's not fair!"
A deep sigh from under the stairs, "Life's not fair."
"It should be fair... I hate you! I never asked to be born!"
Thumps of my heavy-as-possible feet on the stairs, as if I could trample on Dad's head on the way to fling myself on my bed and cry for ever.

I can't recall what I was so upset about, but I distinctly remember the utter certainty that my dad was wrong. Life *should* be fair. When it wasn't, my parents should *make* it fair rather than simply accepting it. And they certainly shouldn't expect me to accept "life's not fair" as an excuse for injustice. I didn't think things through so clearly back then. All I knew was that it was *wrong*.

Why was I so certain? All the fairy stories end up with the 'bad' characters getting their comeuppance and the 'good' characters living happily ever after. Children's books used to have similar unequivocal moral messages. One of my favourite books at the time was *The Naughtiest Girl in the School* by Enid Blyton — the naughtiest girl sees the error of her ways and becomes a model student, and has so much more fun. Movies and TV programmes were the same. Even history was sanitised for children. Richard the Lionheart went off to the Crusades to fight heroically for God, Bad King John was nasty to everyone but Richard came back, sorted him out and everyone was happy.

It's disappointing to realise that the fictional basis for morality and justice is exactly that — fiction. There are so many counter-examples. Children as young as nine are kidnapped and forced to fight in brutal wars in Africa, Asia, South America, Europe and the Middle East. One-third of British children live in poverty. In Britain, black Caribbean and Pakistani babies are twice as likely to die in their first year as white British babies. How is anyone supposed to remain optimistic about the future of the human race in the face of such inhumanity? More to the point, is there anything we, as individuals, can do to improve conditions?

Early in my own childhood I realised I didn't understand other people. They were often inconsistent, unreasonable, stupid, and downright illogical. Effective social interaction was beyond me, perhaps because not having a TV put me so far outside popular culture I had no frame of reference within which to talk to other children. Adults weren't much better, they were rarely interested in what was going on in my head, and the stuff in their heads appeared to be just dull.

In my childish analysis, it seemed that if you worked hard and were kind to other people, or at the very least didn't harm anyone else, you'd have a good life... that's (arguably) how it *should* be. I soon realised it is not how it was. I raged against the machine throughout my teenage years. I joined the Communist Party, the Anti-Nazi League and CND. I tried to join Exit — the society for voluntary euthanasia — but they wouldn't have me, as I wasn't yet eighteen. I went on marches and wrote letters and petitioned my MP. Nothing seemed to make any difference.

My parents were right, life wasn't fair. And by the time I left school I was convinced there was no point trying to make it fair. My slogan (which I wrote on numerous walls in the Reading suburb where I grew up) was: "Life is futile".

In my mid-twenties I became a parent myself. I hadn't planned to, in fact, I'd always been adamant that I was never going to have children. Then my treacherous hormones let me down. It wasn't a good idea, as I had no conception (haha!) of what being a mother involved.

So, I produced two sons. I was determined not to make the same 'mistakes' as my own parents, although I wasn't quite sure what those had been. I wanted my children to grow up with a sense of security, self-belief and optimism, rather than the boredom, disenchantment and depression I'd somehow acquired. I read all the books. And I mean *all* the books. I joined a Usenet group[1] — misc.kids — and argued with right-wing Americans about whether returning to work after having children would be the worst fate I could visit on my offspring. I discussed potential parenting problems with my ex-husband, my friends (none of whom were the least bit interested in having children) and my parents (who wisely declined to comment).

All the advice I did manage to glean seemed to go along the lines of:

1. Patience is the most important quality you will need. Your children will drive you to distraction, and you must be endlessly patient and loving.
2. Consistency is also the most important quality you will need. Even a minor slip in behavioural patterns will result in major problems later on.
3. Reward good behaviour, ignore bad behaviour. Always praise the behaviour, never label the child.
4. Sleep when the baby sleeps. You will want to devote all your waking hours to your new role as a mother, and you won't mind that time for yourself will be a thing of the past.
5. It may be tough at times, but you will enjoy every moment you spend with your offspring. Being a parent is the most rewarding activity possible.
6. ... *ad nauseum*.

No wonder I ended up with post-natal depression. Which was lucky in one way, because it led to my health visitor giving me the most important piece of advice on being a

[1] Online forums that existed before the World Wide Web

parent I ever received: "You will never be a perfect mother. The best you can achieve is to be a 'good enough' mother."

It's probably best to draw a veil over the baby/toddler years. Some people like tiny human beings. I don't. I couldn't wait for them to learn to talk properly, to have a real conversation rather than repeating "Why?" until it was impossible to restrain myself from screaming "Just because!" at the top of my voice, then breaking down into guilty sobs.

Despite my intolerance of the little buggers, I did have a fierce need to protect them from the worst the world might throw at them. They weren't going to go through the state school system, that was for sure. My ex-husband didn't have a problem with sending them to an independent school — he is an unrepentant Tory voter. I thought I would struggle with it, but the truism that "it's different when it's your own children" proved accurate. What difference would it make to state education if the boys weren't part of it? Not much, I reasoned. Principles be damned — life isn't fair, so I was going to make sure my kids were on the "right" side of the balance.

Of course, I couldn't protect them from everything. My younger son, Blake, was skinny and weird, so was intermittently bullied at school from an early age. There was one time in particular, when a lad in Blake's class had been quite vicious towards Blake and some of the kids in the year below. Blake told me about it, then we told his teacher, and the school immediately put a stop to it. From then on, the younger kids worshipped him as a hero. I made sure he was aware of what he'd done and how proud I was of the stand he'd taken. I don't think it was as clear in my mind then, but what I was doing was teaching him he can make a difference, at least some of the time.

A couple of years after that incident I had a text message from Blake, who was away at summer camp at the time. He'd made friends with a girl who was being bullied by another group of kids, to the extent that they'd framed her for stealing. He was distraught that he couldn't do anything to help her. My advice was to stand by her, make sure she knew he didn't doubt her, maybe talk to the camp staff if she was willing... his response was, "Yes, I know all that, but how can I fix it so this isn't happening?" Difficult question. How could I tell my son that life's not fair and people can be vile, without instilling a sense of life's futility in him? After thinking about it for a while, I realised I was learning from him, rather than the other way round. It isn't possible for one person to fix the world, or even a significant part of it. But it *is* possible to make a difference in individual lives, and for Blake's friend, the fact that he believed in her has, I hope, made a significant difference to *her* world.

Blake has been lucky to find a group of friends who are as geeky as he is, which has helped him develop into a well-adjusted seventeen-year-old who is happy and proud to stand up for what he believes. He hasn't had a particularly easy life, but he's maintained his right to be as he is and not conform to societal expectations. He regularly comments on current affairs, showing the same level of outrage I still have about the apparent idiocy of most of the human race. However, rather than trying to fix everything all at once, he tackles issues that are within his capability to resolve. He doesn't think it's unusual that he will always stand up for his friends against bullies — he doesn't understand how anyone would consider behaving otherwise. I think this quiet caring attitude towards humanity is just as necessary to making a better place as the need to tear down the structures that are destroying the world.

Simon, my older son, is bright and ever-so-slightly geeky, but he has always been popular, surrounded by friends. Because of this he's been able to get away with coasting through life. He's somehow got in the habit of telling convenient lies to stave off the consequences of his laziness or thoughtlessness, which is extremely frustrating to deal with. If he was inherently more lazy and thoughtless than any other teenage boy, I'd probably have throttled him by now.

Simon has always used his status among other kids to be helpful. He's one of the few lads I know who will actively step in to stop unfair behaviour or speak out against prejudice or idiocy. Like Blake, he has a clear idea of right and wrong, of how to behave towards other people, but unlike the younger Blake, he has always had the confidence to stand up for his beliefs. He's lacking direction at the moment, but I think once he works out what he wants to do there will be no stopping him. And whatever that is, it will involve helping and supporting other people, and making a difference in his own part of the world.

When I became a parent, everything was raised to a new level of significance. A thoughtless remark that might upset a friend or send a partner into a huff for a couple of days could turn my child into a permanently dysfunctional human being. I overthink small issues to the point of obsession (does it make me a bad mother to buy crisps for them to snack on?) and the big issues feed on me in the dark hours of the night. Should I be taking them on protest marches and encouraging them to get involved in practical ways to change the world? Perhaps we should have joined the Occupy Nottingham protest camp, or at least gone along to their meetings? But, the most important lesson I've taught them is to be accepting of others' differences and to take a stand against injustice. The moment I knew I'd done a good job was when I sat them down and told them that I'm gay. Simon said, "Is that all? Can I go out now?" and Blake said, "You looked so serious, I was expecting something bad." They both gave me a hug and went about their business.

I'm proud of both my sons. They're different from each other, but in their own ways they're considerate and optimistic young men. Neither of them sees the world through rose-tinted glasses, but rather than focusing on the doom and gloom (as I did at their age) they see the possibilities. They accept their limitations — neither is destined for a stellar career in cancer research, international diplomacy or saving the environment, but both quietly go about changing the world around them in whatever way they can. Perhaps if everyone on the planet was more like them, humanity would be in a much better state. And, as a parent, I can't ask for more than that.

The World Turned Upside Down

Leon Rosselson

In sixteen forty-nine, to St George's Hill,
A ragged band they called the Diggers came to show the
people's will,
They defied the landlords, they defied the laws,
They were the dispossessed reclaiming what was theirs.

We come in peace, they said, to dig and sow,
We come to work the lands in common and to make the waste
ground grow,
This earth divided, we will make whole,
So it will be a common treasury for all.

The sin of property we do disdain,
No man has any right to buy and sell the earth for private gain,
By theft and murder, they took the land,
Now everywhere the walls spring up at their command.

They make the laws to chain us well,
The clergy dazzle us with heaven or they damn us into hell,
We will not worship the god they serve,
The god of greed who feeds the rich while poor folk starve.

We work, we eat together, we need no swords,
We will not bow to the masters or pay rent to the lords,
Still we are free, though we are poor,
You Diggers all stand up for glory, stand up now.

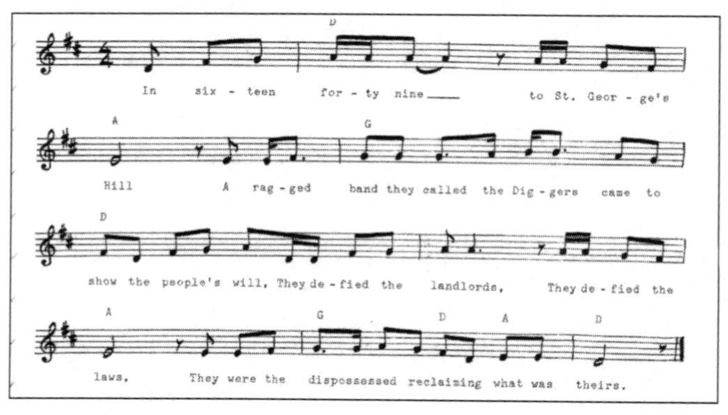

From the men of property, the orders came,
They sent the hired men and troopers to wipe out the
    Diggers' claim,
Tear down their cottages, destroy their corn,
They were dispersed — but still the vision lingers on:

You poor take courage, you rich take care,
This earth was made a common treasury for everyone to share,
All things in common, all people one,
We come in peace — the orders came to cut them down.

Bringing the News from Nowhere

Leon Rosselson

Some bring the news in a sermon on the mountain
And some bring the news in a blueprint or a bulletin
But I like those who come with the passion of a vision
Like a child with a gift, like a friend with a question.
William Morris was one.
In a story, in a song,
In the patterns that he wove, in the colours that he loved,
In the hope that he gave, he brought the news
From nowhere.

In my mind's eye I can see him still standing
With his grey beard waving like the foam of the sea,
With his shaggy hair shaking and his clear eyes shining
As he tells all who listen how different life could be.
And he rages at the wealthy with their mutilated vision,
Making money the measure for everything they do,
And the ugliness that kills and the lives that are broken
On the wheels that turn for the profits of the few.

And some bring the news...

So he turned from his class and he made the lonely journey
Through the river of fire, and when he reached the other side
He joined the ones who had nothing, the poor and the hungry,
And their cause was his till the day that he died.
For he saw that in them a spark lay hidden
And he saw that in them a hope still burned
For the great change coming when the shoddy rule of Mammon
Would be shattered like a hulk that the storm has overturned.

And some bring the news...

When our desires are freed, he said, there'll be no schools or prisons,
No parliaments or leaders to coerce us with their laws,
No property, no money to raise false divisions,
And there can be an end to the endlessness of wars.
And work will be a sharing and work will be a pleasure
When the things we make are born out of beauty and of need.
In a world made whole, he said, we all can be creators,
Not winners and losers in a game of grab and greed.
And some bring the news...

He took delight and he looked with eyes of wonder
At the skin and the body and the beauty of the earth.
We must cherish the fields and the woods and the rivers,
For if we defile our home, he said, what then will life be worth?
And some there were who said he was just another dreamer
But his dream danced on though the years turned to stone,
And his dream shimmers still like the sunlight in winter
For a dream is the door to a world unknown.

So honour to the man and honour to the dreamer
And to all the men and women the history books ignore
Who would not turn aside for the bribes and the clamour
But held to the hope in the vision that they saw.

And some bring the news...

Welsh Utopia: Shelley at Tremadoc

Ian Parks

When I lived in North Wales in the mid-1990s I often passed through the village of Tremadoc on my way to and from work. As far as I knew its only claim to fame was as the birthplace of T.E. Lawrence. There was a portrait of him, resplendent in robes, by Augustus John above the bar in the local pub. Then, one late autumn afternoon, as I sat drinking there, the landlord, who'd heard I was a poet, asked me if I knew that Shelley had lived in a house nearby. I downed my pint and, equipped with directions, set off uphill through the rain. It was a steady climb: on one side the hillside rose steeply, the dank earth held in place by the exposed roots of trees; on the other were glimpses of the village and beyond it, Cardigan Bay. I turned into a drive and there it was: whitewashed, foursquare, with a roof of local grey slate. It still bore the name it had when Shelley lived there between September 1812 and February 1813: Tan-yr-Allt, which means, appropriately, the house under the hill. There was nobody about.

The only indication that Shelley had lived there was a plaque of the same Welsh slate outside the main door inscribed with a line from *Queen Mab* — the long philosophical poem the poet had written during his sojourn there. Whoever had chosen that line — 'All things are recreated' — knew their Shelley well, as themes of renewal and regeneration in both nature and human affairs run through the whole of his work as a poet. I'd been told that the house was now a Steiner School, something I felt Shelley would have approved of, and I approached expecting to hear the sound of children. The school itself seemed to be deserted but the door was open so I went in, hoping to meet a teacher, secretary or caretaker who would perhaps let me have a look around. I rang the bell and after a long wait a young woman came down the stairs and into the hall. It was her first job, she told me. She hadn't read any Shelley herself or even heard of him until she came to work at the school, but she knew all there was to know about his stay there. She took me into a bright, airy classroom with books and cushions scattered on the floor and paintings by children on the walls. 'This,' she said, 'was Shelley's drawing room.' Not knowing what to say I nodded approval. 'And this is the hole made by the pistol ball when they tried to kill him.' I was surprised at what she'd said but there, in the panelling on the far side of the room was a splintered hole torn into the wood. Why would anyone want to kill a poet?

Shelley, aged twenty-one, arrived in North Wales after a period of itinerant wandering with his young wife Harriet that had taken them recently to Keswick, Lynmouth and Dublin, where the poet had been active in supporting the cause of Irish Republicanism. It was a strange time to wash up there: a giant of a man was on the run after murdering a local woman and the Caernarvon peninsula had recently been alight with political agitation and unrest. The landscape itself was bleak and forbidding; the isolation in a time of poor communications and lack of transport immediate and real. What Shelley came across by chance compelled him to stay. Tremadoc, which remains by and large unchanged, was only recently built, an experiment in community planning by one W.A. Madock, who constructed it along Owenite principles as a purpose-built, self-sufficient working village and named it after himself. The thinking behind it was similar to principles that were later to inform the construction of Saltaire, the model village near Bradford, by mill owner Titus Salt. Here, perhaps, was the new start that Shelley had been searching for and he threw himself into the New Town and Embankment project with the manic enthusiasm he so often displayed when animated by some fresh idea or opportunity. He secured the rent of Tan-yr-Allt from Madock even though his reputation had preceded him and the landlord had been warned of Shelley's proclivity for disappearing without paying his debts. The advice — which proved to be sound as records show that Shelley ran up substantial debts while living at Tan-yr-Allt — was ignored by Madock who seems to have been flattered by the poet's interest in the project and keen to ellicit his help. Central to the success of the scheme was the construction of a huge embankment across the mouth of the estuary and the reclamation of the land beyond it. Over a hundred men were involved in the building of the Cob, which had collapsed dramatically earlier in the year and was in the process of being rebuilt. Shelley visited daily, spoke eloquently at local gatherings intended to raise money for the project — and made enemies. Among them were local landowners who supplied materials and manpower for the building of the Cob, and participants in the project who resented Shelley's interference and his overt radicalisation of the scheme. The most prominent of these, a man named Leeson, was handed one of the seditious tracts Shelley had been disseminating in Ireland. Of all the local interests in Tremadoc, he had the most to lose if Shelley's radical ideas were spread among the workforce. The available evidence indicates that Shelley wanted not merely to take part in the project but to direct it along strongly egalitarian lines with the formation of unions and better pay and conditions for the workers. Shelley, who at first appeared to be an asset to the project, very soon looked as if he might become a liability, contributing to its failure and threatening its viability.

Shelley's enthusiasm about the creation of an ideal society in the wilds of North Wales was mirrored in the poetry he wrote during his stay at Tremadoc. *Queen Mab* represented a significant move forward in Shelley's development as a poet. In it he abandoned the arch romanticism that informed his earlier work and attempted something on a more ambitious scale. Although the poem is of interest in itself, the extensive notes that accompany it as a commentary set out Shelley's ideas of a utopian society — or rather his thoughts on the established and received ideas that stood in the way of its realisation. Shelley was a notorious and outspoken atheist and atheistic principles inform the whole of the poem, as do his ideas on the equality of the sexes, egalitarianism, vegetarianism (then viewed as an eccentricity) and vehement republicanism derived from the thinking of Godwin and Tom Paine. Most of these ideas were highly inflammatory at a time when government fears of revolution were running high and drastic measures were being taken to root out radicalism wherever it was found. The ideas contained in *Queen Mab* were regarded as being so dangerous that Shelley's publishers faced prosecution for printing it. Consigned to the back pages of collected editions of Shelley's work, along with the Juvenilia, the poem receives little attention today and seems to have found few readers during the poet's lifetime. Shelley often expressed his bitter disappointment at the lack of acknowledgement it received and never lived to see its rise in popularity during the two decades after his death, when it was taken up by a new generation of radicals, becoming known eventually as 'the Chartist Bible'.

While Shelley was working on *Queen Mab* at Tan-yr-Allt during the first two months of 1813 things were coming to a head. What transpired on the stormy, rain-drenched night of 26th/27th February is sinister, sensational, and difficult to substantiate. Events seem to have been triggered by the arrival on the 26th of Shelley's Irish manservant Dan Healey, who had been arrested in Barnstaple for disseminating seditious pamphlets authored by Shelley, and had just been released from prison after serving a sentence of six months. Shelley had long been convinced that he was being followed by spies — a claim which is not as outrageous as it first appears — and it is possible that someone in the pay of the government had tracked Healey to Tremadoc in the hope of locating his master. The exact sequence of events is impossible to determine. According to Harriet, whose sister was now staying with the Shelleys at Tan-yr-Allt, 'we returned to bed between ten and eleven o'clock' and were woken 'within the hour by 'a noise proceeding from one of the parlours.' Shelley 'immediately went down stairs with two pistols, which he had laded that night, expecting to have occasion for them'. The implication that Shelley was expecting trouble either from Leeson, government spies, or another, unidentified source, is obvious. Harriet's account is, as one would expect, confused. She, after all, only heard the events from upstairs and was not a witness to them. However, between her account and that of her husband, it is possible to infer that Shelley disturbed an intruder exiting the house through the French windows fronting on the lawn, that he used one of his pistols which misfired, and then became in some sort of scuffle with the man outside the house which resulted in them rolling on the ground. Whoever the intruder was, it seems likely that his intention was to gather incriminating papers rather than to attack Shelley or his family. The possibility that Shelley's second pistol was fired and wounded the intruder is reinforced by the fact that he disappeared into the night threatening vengeance: he would murder Shelley and rape his wife and sister.

Three hours elapsed with Shelley in 'an agitated state'. Tan-yr-Allt is isolated now and would have been more so at the beginning of the nineteenth century. To send for help would have meant risking injury or death to whoever ventured out of the house. Around four o'clock the intruder, or one who two others sent by him returned. A shot or two were fired through the windows, shattering them, passing through Shelley's nightshirt but not hitting him, and ending up embedded in the panelling. The attack lasted for no longer than a few seconds and it is impossible to identify the assailants or to divine whether the intention was to kill Shelley or merely intimidate him.

If the motive was to intimidate, it had the desired effect. The next day the poet wrote urgently to his friends John and Leigh Hunt, reclaiming a recent subscription of twenty pounds to the latter who had been sentenced for libel. 'I have,' wrote Shelley, 'escaped an atrocious assassination.' Harriet added a postscript of her own: 'Shelley,' she said, 'was dreadfully nervous' and she was of the opinion that 'our lives are not safe as long as we remain.' The money was used to finance their escape from Tremadoc. The family was to return briefly to Dublin from where Shelley sent the manuscript of *Queen Mab* to his publisher in London where it appeared in 1813.

It is difficult to know what to make of this bizarre episode. Some commentators have suggested that Shelley — unstable at the best of times and in a nervous state — was hallucinating, exaggerating, or merely inventing the story to provide a convenient excuse to explain his hasty departure from Tremadoc where he had either grown disillusioned with the project or needed to avoid his creditors. If this is the case, it means we have to question Harriet's independent testimony and her record of the events. Shelley was later to make a drawing of his assailant that night. It is an image of childlike simplicity. The sketch is scrappy but the intruder appears to be naked — a horned, grinning, malevolent, fiendish creature with arms that bear a striking resemblance to branches (Tan-yr-Allt is surrounded by trees). It may well be a representation of Shelley's subjective impression of his assailant; it would certainly be useless were it used in an attempt to identify the real perpetrators of an assassination attempt. Given the nature of the evidence, the length of time that has passed, the temperament of the poet, the circumstances he found himself in, and the cult that has built up around the person of Shelley, it is impossible to know for sure what transpired. More significant than the sinister events of that stormy night, however, is the strong connection that exists between the writing of *Queen Mab* and Shelley's activities at

Tremadoc: while he was contemplating the possibility of an ideal society through the composition of the poem he was engaged in an attempt to create a semblance of it in a remote corner of North Wales. It constitutes a neglected period in the life of Shelley and of his development as a thinker and a poet.

After looking around the school I strolled to the bottom of the sloping lawn in the direction from which Shelley's assailant had approached the house. The lights were being turned on in the upstairs rooms. I took a moment to think of Shelley's eventful winter there and of the poem he produced while being embroiled in the troubled attempt to build a Welsh utopia.

I've never been back since. Later that year I moved to Oxford where Shelley had been enrolled briefly as a student at University College. Oxford had wanted nothing to do with Shelley, expelling him for publishing a pamphlet called *The Necessity of Atheism*. And Shelley, evidently, had wanted nothing to do with Oxford either, abandoning his formal studies and taking up an itinerant and erratic lifestyle which was to continue until his death in 1822. Only after that death and the subsequent rehabilitation of Shelley as a poet of nature and love did his old college try to make a claim on him, commissioning the white marble statue of the drowned Shelley washed up on the shore at Viareggio — more of an incorruptible god of classical mythology than a dead human — surrounding it with a railing and placing it under a dome. It is a far remove from the rugged Welsh hillside overlooking the sea, but if the spirit of Shelley persists anywhere it is more likely to do so there than among the spires and quadrangles of a city he despised.

Freedom without Territory

David Rosenberg

Oscar Wilde famously argued that a map of the word that does not include Utopia "is not worth even glancing at". But is it possible for an oppressed, excluded and endangered people to imagine leaping into a world of freedom and establishing their Utopia without reference to a map or borders?

The 20th century was a century of paradox. Stupendous advances in science and technical innovation occurred alongside war and destruction on a colossal scale. But it was also a century of democracy and freedom, of independence movements and national liberation struggles as people fought for self-determination. Their success was graphically demonstrated as newly independent states unfurled bright new flags, displayed new national symbols, introduced new currencies bearing new leaders' faces. Some even adopted new languages.

In 1930's Poland, Europe's largest Jewish community dreamt of their liberation too. Poland's 3.3 million Jews comprised a tenth of the country's population. Jews had lived there for at least 800 years. In some cities, including the capital, Warsaw, more than a third of the population were Jews. By the mid-1940s, though, Poland was the world's biggest Jewish cemetery.

And yet, just a few years before that catastrophe, a vibrant and revolutionary political and cultural movement came to the fore in Poland's Jewish life. It swept the Jewish vote in municipal and communal elections, dared to imagine a Utopia, and even began to build it.

This was not the Jewish nationalist movement that spoke of liberation but sought to transplant its "promised land" on to someone else's territory in Palestine. On the contrary, this radical movement in 1930's Poland subscribed to a diasporic concept of *doikayt* (hereness) and sought to liberate the Jews where they were. Their propaganda posters proclaimed: "Here, where we live, is our homeland." They did not want a new flag or their own army to defend borders. They wanted to disband armies and they refused to ape the nationalists who had oppressed them, or adopt their values of "might is right". Emanuel Scherer, an activist within this movement, summed up their outlook: "Rights and justice for Jews everywhere without wrongs and injustice to other people anywhere."

They wanted to arm the people not with guns but with a humanistic philosophy of freedom, internationalism and enlightenment, a powerful sense of self-worth and collective strength, while creating the economic means to satisfy the material hunger of a population enduring widespread poverty. The new world they imagined would not differ from the old by adding a new name on a map, but in the very nature of the human beings that inhabited it and how they related to each other. According to the American scholar, Jack Jacobs, their struggle was not just to improve conditions but to create *naye mentshen* — new people.

That movement called itself the *Bund*. It is a Yiddish word that means to join together — like the word "bind" in English. The people it sought to bind together were mainly impoverished workers living in overcrowded city tenements and crumbling houses in small towns and villages. Prohibited by discriminatory laws from working in government-owned enterprises, they populated workshops and factories making clothes and textiles, leather and metal goods; they worked as boot and shoemakers, or as carpenters — not manufacturing luxury goods but making everyday necessities. Discrimination also limited their educational opportunities, though their families, if faced with a choice between glittering university careers for their children and the possibility of them leaving school to earn much needed income for the family in the here and now, would invariably have chosen the latter.

A small proportion of Polish Jews owned the businesses

that most of their co-religionists worked in; another small proportion were entering the professions. In an atmosphere of rising anti-semitism, government ministers openly advocated "economic discrimination, by all means" against the Jews, while hypocritically condemning fellow Poles who physically attacked and abused Jews.

Jews were excluded and isolated but not completely friendless. The Bund had good relations with socialists among other national minorities in Poland's cities — Lithuanians, Ukrainians and, indeed, the Germans. The Polish Socialist Party (PPS) also sought a better future for Poland's workers, but was factionally divided. Its nationalist right wing was less sympathetic to Jews, but its left wing worked closely with the Bund. It was only where Polish Socialists were elected to town councils that Jews could access local council employment.

If external circumstances were unpromising, the Jewish community's internal life posed other problems. As Jews were increasingly exposed to the unfolding secularising processes of modern urban life, religious leaders of the community, who had resisted modernity and the Enlightenment, talked of sins and transgressions, and condemned any free thought. Rabbis still held great sway, controlling many of the institutions that Jews of all ages regularly came into contact with.

The Bund had been formed in 1897 through struggles for workers' rights in areas of the Tsarist Russian Empire that then included Poland. It recruited Jews into trade unions, formed self-defence squads against marauding anti-semites perpetrating pogroms, and fought in the revolutionary upheavals of 1905 and 1917. The fortunes of the 20th century left rose and fell with Bolshevism and social democracy. Totalitarianism gathered pace under early Bolshevik leaders even before Stalin. Social democracy made gains for workers in Western countries but made compromises with capitalism. The Bund, however, was a living testament to a vibrant and radical "third road" socialism. It fought tenaciously for reforms, campaigning for every measure that would bring even a temporary amelioration of workers' conditions, but rejected reformism as a strategy for change. It fought a class struggle for workers' control of society but opposed the dictatorship of a new political class over the workers' party, as had occurred in Russia. For the Bund, socialism without democracy was inconceivable. Though any direct contact was most improbable, the Gandhian idea that "you must be the change you want in the world" lived passionately in the hearts of Eastern European Bundists.

When Poland became independent again in 1919, it was home to the former empire's largest Jewish population and provided the stage on which the Bund sought to create a new world. The horrors later inflicted on Jews during the Nazi occupation of Poland and surrounding lands decimated the Bund. Branches of the organisation elsewhere, founded by émigrés before the catastrophe, survived, but its heart was ripped out. I was fortunate to have had the chance to talk with a few of the survivors who described the life, the vision and their attempts to build a new existence. Each Bundist I met told me that their dreams rested above all with the next generation starting to harness the new political and cultural possibilities that older Bundists had begun to create.

On the eve of the Second World War, 12,000 young Polish Jews were members of a Bundist youth organisation called *Tsukunft* — Yiddish for "Future". The Nazis' efforts to eradicate a Jewish future were more than metaphorical. Thousands more, aged between ten and sixteen, were members of the Bund's children's organisation, *Sotsialistisher Kinder Farband* (SKIF). After being called up for nineteen months army service at the beginning of the 1930s, Majer Bogdanski, a tailor from Piotrkow, spent the rest of that decade as a trade union activist among clothing workers and as a Bundist organiser in the industrial city of Lodz. Though small in stature he was renowned for his fiery speeches. When I asked him to recall the finest moments of the Bund he didn't talk firstly about the strikes against slave-driving employers, the daily fight for work for the unemployed, the frequent and bloody street battles with anti-semites, or mass May Day marches where Jewish and non-Jewish workers felt their collective strength; instead he talked of time spent with the Bund's youngest followers.

"Life was hard but it also had very beautiful moments," said Majer. "With the youth organisation and the children's organisation we organised summer camps and dances. The children were particularly interesting and nice to be with. They would organise summer camps which we called Socialist Children's Republics, and they learned to live together as socialists. We considered this the crown of our year's work. Not one child would be allowed to leave SKIF, when they were grouped over to the Youth Organisation (*Tsukunft*) at the age of sixteen, without having been to such a camp at least once."

Perec Zylberberg grew up with his older brother David and younger sister Esther in a respected Bundist family in Lodz. His mother was an organiser for *Yidishe Arbete Froyen*, the Bundist women's organisation, and his father was a master weaver in a factory, and a leader within the textile workers' trade union. Perec enrolled in his local SKIF branch. By 1939, there were 750 *Skifistn* in Lodz alone. During the war Perec survived incarceration in Teresienstadt concentration camp. He and just four others from those 750 child Bundists survived the Holocaust. He recalled attending a SKIF camp on the banks of the River Vileyka not far from Vilna (Vilnius) where the Bund had first come into existence: "These were turbulent times. Anti-semitic gangs and even political parties engaged in Jew-bashing activities. But we were full of zest. The first experience of living in a children's republic was exhilarating. We were getting into the real spirit of comradely inspired living."

Perec's younger sister Esther survived Auschwitz and Bergen-Belsen death camps. Her formal education ended when she was just eleven years old, as her family were imprisoned in the Lodz ghetto. At the age of three or four she started her schooling at the Grosser kindergarten — Grosser was one of the Bund's founders — and from there Esther enrolled in the Medem *Shule*, a secular Yiddish-oriented school, part of a network of radical, secular, Jewish schools that Bundists and like-minded people created in inter-war Poland.

Esther's school was named after the remarkable Vladimir Medem. In spite of his parents' conversion from Judaism to Christianity, Medem became a Bund ideologue and articulated its key idea of "non-territorial national cultural autonomy". Medem promoted the idea of a "state of nationalities" in which citizenship would be nationally neutral and granted equally to members of all nationalities. It was an alternative model to the traditional nation state and the territorial nationalism and majoritarianism that usually accompanied it. It obliged the state to support the cultural autonomy of minorities, but emphasised "peoplehood" more than statehood. Rather than elevating community leaders of minority groups, it was about cultural equality for ordinary people of all communities. Even today it stands as a radical version of progressive multiculturalism.

Children attending the Medem *Shule* were taught entirely in their Yiddish mother tongue during their first year. Polish was introduced later, especially for teaching Polish history, but Jewish history was taught in Yiddish. "Nothing was compulsory," Esther recalled. "The school was run on free and democratic lines. When I talk to my children and ask them how do you look back on your school years, there is very little there that draws them back, but I remember all my teachers with absolute devotion and love. There was something very special about the school, maybe because we felt that as little people we mattered. We knew they cared very much. At the Medem *Shule* we had no such thing as a religious assembly. The other schools did but it wasn't forced upon us. We had a school hymn: *"Lomir zingen a lid tsu der yiddisher shule, vos iz alemen undz azoy tayer. Lomir zingen mit freyd un mit hofnung ful, oyf a velt, a fraye a naye."* (Let us sing a song to the Yiddish school, which is dear to us all. Let us sing full of hope and joy for a new and free world.)

The Medem *Shule* was one of the few co-educational schools in Poland at that time: Esther remembers "a great sense of equality in our school. We had men and women teachers and this was very progressive at the time. When they taught the Hebrew prophets, they taught not just in terms of what they were saying would happen but what was right to do. This school gave me a very strong feeling of what was right and what was just and how to conduct oneself in life — how to be a free human being. We managed to carry it within us and it helped me in the ghetto in the darkest hours of the war. I have always retained this belief in my fellow human beings."

The democratic, humanistic values of the school were replicated within another remarkable institution that the Bund created through members' subscriptions and wider support from Bund-affiliated trade unions and supporters abroad. In Poland's biggest cities where workers lived in cramped unsanitary conditions, tuberculosis was rampant. In 1926 the Bund founded a sanatorium in a rural location outside of Warsaw, where victims of TB aged between six and sixteen could recuperate, on average staying for ten weeks. Users took responsibility for decision-making. Supported by adult staff, children at the sanatorium governed themselves, gardened, cared for farm animals and bees, participated in science lessons, sport and singing entertainments, and learned to live in a socialist way that emphasised freedom, independence and cooperation. Many teachers at the sanatorium had taught previously in Bundist schools, and techniques of learning through cooperative play tested at the sanatorium later fed back into those schools.

Like the school that Esther attended this sanatorium also bore the name "Medem" while other significant Bundists were similarly honoured by having institutions named after them. These included drama groups, libraries and sports organisations that the Bund created, as it sought to widen horizons and foster new cultural opportunities among the poorest sectors of society. Yet Bundist survivors confirm that the relationship between leaders and followers of the Bund remained true to the party's egalitarian spirit. Leon Kuczynski, a grassroots Bund activist in Warsaw in the 1930s, who was frequently involved in physical confrontations to defend Jews from rampaging anti-semites, spoke glowingly to me of Henryk Erlich and Victor Alter, the two most prominent Bundist leaders then. He insisted that "ordinary working class people looked up to Erlich and Alter but they never looked down on us. They listened to us. In other parties the leaders led and the others followed." Majer Bogdanski remembered how Bundists recoiled with discomfort when they saw images from the Spanish Civil War of Party leaders' portraits being carried by marching socialists. "We never venerated our leaders," he says. "We loved them, but we would never carry their pictures on demonstrations."

It was in the Bund's attention to culture that the seeds of their Utopia could perhaps already be seen to be growing before the Holocaust. Majer Bogdanski confirmed that although the workplace was a source of painful exploitation, Bundists never sought to escape their role as producers for more comfortable managerial roles or to become bosses themselves. "We wanted to be *educated* workers," he explained. For people like Majer, apprenticed to work at thirteen years old, culture and education were treasures. The Bund's daily newspaper, the *Folkstsaytung* not only held up a mirror to workers' lives and experiences and connected their daily struggles with those taking place elsewhere in the country and around the world, but provided a platform too for writers and poets. The Bund's cultural initiatives transformed their members' quality of life and self-esteem, just as much as successful trade union activism.

The conventional wisdom of historians of Bundism is that it rose to a hegemonic position among Polish Jewry in the late 1930s because of its leading role in the fight against anti-semitism, a fight never seriously engaged in by Zionists who concentrated instead on training a young elite for life in Palestine, and a fight in which religious leaders offered little more than empty promises that God would intervene to save the Jews. But Jack Jacobs has posed a fascinating alternative explanation, which highlights the impact of the Bund's cultural activity in so many spheres, and singles out especially the role of Bund-initiated discussion groups that had mushroomed among young people, which delved into topics such as sexual taboos, free love, prostitution, and birth control.* For youth heavily influenced by religious leaders on these matters, the discussion groups brought enlightenment

Members of *Morgnshtern*, the Bundist sports organisation

---

* Jack Jacobs, *Bundist Counterculture in Inter-War Poland,* Syracuse, 2009

and enabled them to envision a new and free society being created within the decaying older one.

There is no doubt that many religious Jews voted for the militant atheists and Marxists of the Bund in Poland's last municipal elections before the Nazi invasion. The fact that Bundists defended synagogues from physical attack was well-known and appreciated but also in this period many young religious Jews began to question their previously firmly-held beliefs. The world the Bund was opening up for them was attractive and fulfilling and many votes for the Bund from this segment were positive ones.

The Bund's Utopia was strangled almost at birth. Polish Jewry's last stand against Nazi occupiers was enacted on the streets of the Warsaw Ghetto. Opposing political factions formed a united ghetto response that combined cultural, spiritual and physical resistance. It is perhaps fitting that the last surviving member of the command group that led the uprising was Marek Edelman, a member of the *Tsukunft* in Warsaw in 1939 whose Bundist beliefs remained with him till his death in 2009. Looking back at the ghetto resistance, Edelman wrote: "We fought for dignity and freedom, not for territory, nor for a national identity." They were not looking to add another name to a map.

The Golden Era of Kibbutz

J. David Simons

I first went to work as a volunteer on a *kibbutz* in Israel in the summer of 1972. High up in the hills on the border with Lebanon, it was a small settlement founded by Americans five years previously. Bob Dylan was rumoured to have also worked there as a volunteer two months before I arrived. However, the members were sworn to secrecy about their celebrity guest and the rumour was never confirmed.

I worked there for one month. I washed dishes, picked avocados, burned the shit off the chicken cages with a flame-thrower. Along with the rest of the small community, I followed the progress of the Bobby Fischer / Boris Spassky world chess championship as if it were the Cold War itself that was being fought. Rockets fired from Lebanon occasionally flew over my head and we were consigned to trenches and shelters for safety. I was nineteen years old, desperately happy and excited by my adventure. I promised myself that one day I would return.

Israel was not the pariah state then that it is now. Back then, the country was between two wars: the Six Day War of 1967, and the Yom Kippur War that was to come the following year. The massacre of Israeli athletes at the Munich Olympics was only weeks away. Israel was the under-dog country in those days, the plucky young David amidst the Goliath Arab states. There was no Intifada. Yasser Arafat and the PLO were the terrorists of the day. It never occurred to my naive young mind that the Palestinians were an oppressed people.

I grew up in Scotland in the Swinging Sixties when going off to live in a communal settlement fitted in with the prevailing *zeitgeist*. My father was an ardent socialist. One of my first childhood memories was back in 1960 marching in a May Day Parade to the local park to hear Paul Robeson make a speech and sing 'Old Man River'. He was the first black person I had ever seen. I wasn't sent to the Boy Scouts but to a socialist Zionist organisation called *Habonim* — Hebrew for 'the builders'. Their ethos was to inspire young Jews to emigrate to Israel where they would help build *kibbutzim*. Golda Meir, Mike Leigh and Sacha Baron Cohen are famous *Habonim* alumni. It was therefore no surprise to myself that I kept my promise.

Six years after my first visit, I gave up my partnership in an Edinburgh law firm and went back to Israel.

This time around, I was sent to a *kibbutz* in the Jordan Valley, just south of the Sea of Galilee, again on the border, this time with Jordan. This settlement was one of the oldest in Israel, founded in 1924 on land purchased on its behalf by Baron Edmond James de Rothschild and his Palestine Jewish Colonisation Association. Some biblical scholars locate the Garden of Eden around the area of this *kibbutz*. I would not be surprised. During the decade I lived and worked there, this place was a true Utopia.

Unlike the American *kibbutz* of my first visit, this *kibbutz* was a mature settlement set against the stunning backdrop of the Jordanian hills that drifted in colour from cream to pink to purple throughout the day. Its territory

Early photo of members of a kibbutz going to work

stretched close to the edge of a rift that went all the way from Lebanon to the Dead Sea and on to Eilat. The members lived in attractive apartments, some in the design of Spanish villas, situated among tall palms, linked by an intricate network of pathways that allowed for easy cycling from one end of the settlement to the other. The gardens were well developed and beautifully landscaped. In the hot nights, the smell of the frangipani blossom was intoxicating.

Socialism was still the underlying ideology of this community of some five hundred souls. It was a case of 'each person giving according to his or her ability, each receiving according to his or her needs.' Everyone had employment, health care, education and a roof over their heads. The Secretariat of the *kibbutz* rotated every two years. General meetings were held every Saturday evening, members worked in management, services, in the fields or in the factory, as well as contributing to community obligations such as guard duty or serving in the dining room. There were communal facilities that included a swimming pool, a basketball court, a cinema and a primary school for the whole of the valley. Members ate communally in the dining room, they celebrated festivals, births, marriages and deaths together. The children were still raised separately away from their families in their own age-groups from birth until they had to enter the Israeli army.

It was a time when the internal socialist structure of the *kibbutz* dovetailed well with the capitalist world outside. The *kibbutz* ran a successful plastics factory which produced shampoo bottles for a well-known American cosmetics company and water bottles for the Army. The *kibbutz* was also part of a Jordan Valley collective which exported dates, avocados, bananas and grapefruit to the outside world. These profits externally gained were shared equally among the membership to provide everyone with an apartment, a TV, a telephone, air-conditioning, the opportunity to study at university or to travel abroad. No-one received a wage, just a small monthly budget with which to purchase little luxuries such as chocolate and branded shampoos at the general store.

For my part, apart from my communal duties, I worked in the date plantations, the cotton fields, the silk-screening department in the factory. I became responsible for irrigating the crops in the valley, the head of the volunteers and eventually taught English at the primary school. I knew everyone on the *kibbutz* and they knew me. I may not have liked everyone and I'm sure not everyone liked me, but I cared for each and every one of them for they were part of my community.

Yes, community. It is amazing how great a motivator community can be. I worked six days a week for months on end, hardly ever stepping out of the *kibbutz*. Even on my Saturday off, more often than not I would have communal duties to fulfil. I received a few monthly shekels for my endeavours yet I was happy to give my unpaid labour in return for everything I needed.

Friday night was the social highpoint of the week when everyone would congregate in the dining room as families for the Sabbath meal. After dinner, there might be a movie or a cultural event from a travelling band of musicians, dancers or theatrical players. Saturday evening was when the general meeting took place where all major issues were discussed. I remember one particular debate which roused many conflicting emotions while summing up for me the essence of this community.

Several years before, one of the young men had decided to leave the *kibbutz* altogether for the city life in Tel Aviv. He had struggled to make a living there, got into trouble with drugs and was eventually arrested for cannabis possession. After serving a short prison sentence, he asked to be allowed to return to live on the *kibbutz*. Much debate was had at the Saturday evening assembly. There was a fear this man could be a bad influence on the rest of the youngsters on the *kibbutz*. There was also a feeling among some that if you left, that was that, and the *kibbutz* shouldn't be seen as a fall-back solution just because you couldn't make it elsewhere. As the debate became more heated, I remember one of the elderly veterans approaching the microphone and saying just three words in Hebrew that concluded the discussion in favour of the young man: '*Hu ben meshek*,' he said.'He is our son.'

I believe this was the golden age of my *kibbutz*. It was a time when its socialist roots had taken its membership to the zenith of communal living while its capitalist success provided for a high level of material comfort. It was also a time when the ideology of the founders still had meaning for their children and their grandchildren.

However, in 1988, at the height of this idyllic synergy, I chose to leave. The first Intifada had started and the Army was beckoning. I was also single, and this *kibbutz* life was ultimately geared up for families and not the roaming bachelor. It was time to move on or I felt I might be marginalised by this community I so loved and admired.

Five years after my departure, the *kibbutz* began to break up. Material success had brought with it the urge to pursue individual ambition rather than the needs of the community. Members wanted to start their own businesses, follow their own career paths. The dairy closed down as did the agricultural branches of cotton and citrus. The housing which had been formerly owned communally was now divided up into private dwellings. Residents became responsible for buying their own food, paying for their electricity and telephone bills. Some of the buildings were turned into accommodation for up-market tourism. The plastics factory remained but mainly employed outside workers. Its profits are still used to fund some of the social services for the residents such as care for the elderly or communal amenities like the swimming pool and the dining room. But hardly anyone eats in the dining room anymore and the building has begun to look shabby and run-down.

It is hard to transmit an ideology. Those principles that

might have inspired you when you were young and even propelled you to establish a successful community are not necessarily the same principles that will appeal to the fourth and fifth generations further down the line. And neither they should be. Each generation has to find its own way, its own values, its own community. The fact that the *kibbutz* was able to survive for as long as it did without having to establish an authoritarian regime to do so, is testament to the many inherent advantages of this kind of system. But I could see the cracks beginning to appear at the end of my own sojourn when greater access to the outside world through television and travel began to seduce the children of the settlement. Over a period of sixty years, the *kibbutz* had grown from a few acres of malaria-infested marshland into a successful society. But in the end, it had to adapt or die.

The *kibbutz* I knew has changed dramatically now. I have so far not found the emotional fortitude to be able to return to see these changes for myself, even after twenty-four years. I am not sure that I will ever want to return to a Utopia that no longer exists.

The Trouble with Happiness

Will Buckingham

It must have been back in around 2004 that I met the happiest man on earth. Contrary to popular rumour, he was not a Buddhist monk. He had not, as far as I know, spent years meditating in a mountainside cave deep in the Himalayas. He did not wear robes the colour of saffron or of claret, nor did he quote lines of ancient scripture from some deep repository of timeless wisdom. Instead, the happiest man on earth was living in a small terraced house, alone, in one of the most apparently troubled areas of Birmingham. And he had a taste for rum.

I should go back a bit and say something about the circumstances of our meeting. Back then, I was living in Birmingham and attempting to make a scant livelihood as a freelance writer. The erratic nature of the work, the impracticability of many of my projects, and the fact that my novel manuscript about a faction of Sanskritist scholar-terrorists based in Poland (the faction was called PIECRUST: The Proto Indo-European Cultural Region Union of Scholar-Terrorists) was yet to hit the big time, all meant that I needed to find other work to supplement my income. So, some time around 2004, I signed up as a researcher on a happiness research project. It was a large project, taking place Europe-wide, everywhere from Århus to Zagreb, and had been funded with a substantial budget from the European Union. As an hourly paid researcher (not much of the substantial budget trickled down to our level, but it was better than no work at all), my job was to wander the outlying regions of Birmingham, knocking on the doors of the elderly, and persuading them to answer a questionnaire about their well-being. If they agreed, I would call back at a later date and subject them to a twenty-page document filled with questions such as these:

— Would you say that you are happy with your life?
— Do you have good friends?
— Do you think that your life has gone well for you?
— Have you got what you wanted to get out of life?
— Have you ever wanted to leave everything behind?
— Do you feel that your life has been a success?

This being science, each question needed to be answered on a scale of one to five, so that the results could be quantified, and so that it would be possible to extrapolate from this mass of data to find out, for example, that Bulgarians were less happy than the Welsh, or that for octogenarian Swedes everything was going swimmingly. I found the research a painful business, in part because of the sheer arduousness of the survey, and in part because I could often see the optimism and general good cheer of those poor old folks who were kindly letting me into their homes and feeding me tea and biscuits begin to dwindle at the sight of the gargantuan survey. *Have you ever wanted to leave everything behind?* Yes, I found myself thinking every day as I returned home on the bus from the outlying regions of Birmingham. Yes…

Nevertheless, that summer, I got to see a lot of Birmingham that I would not otherwise have seen. I pressed on the buzzers of expensive, gated properties on the affluent private boulevards of Sutton Coldfield, and could hear the unmistakable tremors of fear in the voices of those who responded to my buzzing only to tell me to go away. I spent hours in the houses of pensioners on the Castle Vale estate, a huge development built on top of the World War Two airfields, advising residents, who seemed as welcoming as they were reluctant to actually answer any of the survey questions, on how they could best find a reliable plumber using the Yellow Pages, or hearing about what happened to them that day in 1956. And I came to know the streets of Aston.

Back then, Aston was still recovering from an incident the year before when two schoolgirls were killed by machine-gun fire outside a New Year's party. The killing was only the most recent in a history of gang violence in Birmingham — the result of a long-standing turf-war between the Burger Bar Boys and the Johnson crew. Aston, as a result of the shootings, had developed a reputation for violence and lawlessness; and yet the moment I arrived in Aston, I found it more welcoming than almost anywhere else that I carried out this strange research into happiness. Kids played in the streets. People sat out on their steps talking. There was none of that undercurrent of terror, none of that palpable fear of the barbarians slavering at the gates, that you got on those private roads in the more desirable suburbs. Aston, in other words, was a good place to be. It almost made the thankless research in which I was engaged bearable. And it was in Aston that I met the happiest man in the world.

It was one afternoon just after lunch. I had timed my day so that I could just about legitimately claim expenses for lunch, and had spent the morning conducting an interview with an old and slightly world-weary woman who was so clearly unhappy that I could not bear to subject her to the entire questionnaire, so instead I skipped over many of the questions by ticking the boxes that, I guessed, indicated a moderate level of discontent, and tried to keep the interview as brief as possible. I stopped into a sandwich shop for lunch and a coffee, and sat thinking about my Proto Indo-European scholar-terrorists. Then I picked up my bag of questionnaires, and continued my work.

I knocked on the door of his house — one of a terrace of houses, each accessed by a series of three or four steps leading up from the street — and a short, thin, lively-looking old Jamaican man answered. His hair was grey, and he had a disordered beard. He was wearing sandals and shorts and a T-shirt, and he beamed at me in welcome.

— Hello, he said. What can I do for you?
I started telling him about the research. There was a script of sorts that we had for this purpose. We had to say that this was important European Union research. We had to show our badges that indicated that we were affiliated to such-and-such a university. We had to ask if we could make an appointment to come back some other time to interview any old people in the house. But before I had said very much of this, he cut me off.

—Yes, yes, he said, I am sure it is important. Come in, please.
He led me down a Spartan hall with a rattan carpet into the kitchen, and there he pulled out a chair for me. There was a stove in the corner, a sink beside which were piled a few dishes, and some pictures on the walls of sunsets, palm-trees and that kind of thing.

— Sit down, he said.

— Thanks.

— Now, tell me: what are you here for?

— I'm doing a survey on happiness, I said.
My host's eyes opened wide.

— A survey on happiness? he asked. Then he started to giggle.

— On happiness, I said.
He looked at me. I must have looked very earnest, because he just went on laughing.

— They do surveys on happiness? That's a very strange thing.

— I know. It's not *my* research. It's a job I'm doing. I'm trying to find out if anybody here in Aston has time to answer some questions, so we can make an appointment to talk to them.

— I've got time now, he said. Ask me your questions.

— Oh, OK, I said. It will take about forty minutes.

— I have *lots* of time, he chuckled. Biscuits? If it is going to be forty minutes, we will need biscuits.

He got up and went to the cupboard. He returned with a plateful of biscuits. Then he went back to the sink,

opened another cupboard and took out two glasses.
— Drink? he said.
— Water is fine.
— Water? I'm having rum.
— Just water.
He shrugged and filled a glass with water. He brought the glasses — one full and one empty — over to the table and handed the water glass to me. Then he took down a bottle of rum from the shelf and poured himself a drink.
— Cheers, he said. We chinked glasses.

I started on the questionnaire. It began with general questions about age, ethnic group (that curious ontology worthy of a Chinese encyclopaedia in a work by Borges), marital status, sex, employment status and so on. My host answered the questions affably, but with a proneness to giggling that was a little unsettling. It was a hot day. By the time had finished the first few pages, my water-glass was empty.
— Rum? he asked.
— Er, no, I shouldn't. I'm working.
— Just a glass. He filled my glass and grinned at me.
I shrugged and smiled at him.
— OK, just a glass.
We started on the serious questions.
— Would you say that you are happy with your life?
He looked at me strangely, then started to shake with laughter. And I thought that he would say, yes, he was very happy with his life, because he certainly seemed to be very happy with his life. But instead he said this: — Now that is a very stupid question.
Having said this he laughed so hard that I saw tears forming in the corners of his eyes.
— Stupid? I asked.
— What kind of a question is that? he gasped, beating on the table with his fist as if it might help him control his laughter. Who thinks about things like this?

I hesitated, uncertain what to write on the form. Then I ticked the box that indicated, as far as I could tell, that he was very happy. He took another slug of rum.

— Go on, he said. Next question.

— Oh, OK. Do you have good friends?

— I have many friends, he said, topping up his rum.

— Hmm, thanks. Now another question. Do you think that your life has gone well for you?

He frowned and leaned towards me.

— Gone *well*? he said. What does that mean?

He said this in a fashion that was almost Socratic. Has your life *gone well*? What do you mean by *gone well*? And, well — what *did* it mean? I wasn't sure. Was *my* life going well at the moment? I had no idea. No, because my novel about the deranged Sanskritists wasn't going down well at all with the publishers I was sending it to. But then again, yes, because I was here drinking rum in Aston, at two in the afternoon, and beginning to feel far more cheerful about things than I had for a long time. But the survey was about him, not me. I ticked the box marked: *undecided*.

— Next question, I said. Have you got what you wanted to get out of life?

He paused for long enough for me to gulp down the rum. It was thirsty work, this research. He topped me up.

— Got what you *wanted*? Tell me, *who* thinks of these questions?

I waved my hand vaguely in the air.

— Someone, I said. A committee or something. People in universities.

— Very *stupid* people in universities, he said. Then he put his glass of rum down and started to bark with laughter again. Such *very* stupid people, he said.

In this fashion, we spent the hours between two and three o'clock in the afternoon. I made the up the answers as best as I could. I ate biscuits. I drank rum. And in the company of the happiest man on earth, I found that my own sense of gloom and indifference began to dissolve away, until I too was howling with laughter as we enjoyed ourselves poking fun at the authors of the questionnaire, and at those long-faced scholars who spend their time devising questions about well-being, and at the whole damned lot of it.

I don't know whether we ran out of rum first, or whether out meeting was brought to a close by my completion of the form, in an increasingly shaky hand. But eventually I realised it was time to go, and so I put the survey in my bag, my host took me to the door, and there he shook my hand and we thanked each other, laughing. Only then, as I descended the three or four steps down to the street did I realise quite how drunk I was.

Aston seemed a kindly place in the afternoon sunshine. Filled with rum, biscuits and a sense of friendly good cheer, freed from anxious fretting over questions of happiness and unhappiness, I waved goodbye to the happiest man alive, and went to the corner shop to buy some mints, hoping that they might help me sober up before my next interview at four o'clock.

***

Eight years later, in the January of 2012, I published a book on happiness. It was not something that I had planned to write, but as a philosopher-for-hire I was commissioned by Icon Books to write a short, practical introduction to the subject. Given that I am a philosopher by training, when I was asked to write the book, I did so from a philosopher's perspective. And so these were the kinds of questions that I thought it worth exploring: What did Epicurus say about happiness? What about the Stoics? What kinds of things are the various things that we call happiness? Was the ancient Cynic philosopher Diogenes, who was famed for his masturbation in the marketplace, a philosopher of happiness? Is Buddhism really the royal road to calm, peace and fulfilment as its advocates claim? And what are the deeper philosophical problems with the present-day enthusiasm for the notion of happiness in government circles, business, and elsewhere? And because this was supposed to be a practical guide, I set a number of practical exercises so that readers might be able explore the ideas for themselves.

The book, when it was eventually published, was called *Introducing Happiness: a Practical Guide*, which I realised — after the fact — made it sound a bit like a self-help manual, as if I knew what happiness was, and was simply providing twelve useful steps to get there. But, over the years, the reverse has been the case: the more I have thought about happiness, the less I have been certain what it is. If I had had my way, I would have called the book something like, *The Trouble with Happiness: an experimental guide*. But even if I had suggested it, the marketing people would have baulked. The *trouble* with happiness? What trouble? Surely happiness is the end of all troubles…

Surely it is. Yesterday I was troubled, but now my troubles are ended and I am happy. This is, to be sure, a desirable state of affairs. I would like to be happy, by and large; and, by and large, I would like others to be happy as well. Unnecessary trouble is something we could all do without. But at the same time it seems to me that 'happiness' is itself the cause of a great deal of trouble and mischief. After all, Stalin saw himself as a constructor of happiness, and the Red Guards during the cultural revolution sang of how Mao Zedong was the people's happiness: there is often a troubling relationship between tyranny and happiness. There are more subtle kinds of tyranny and trouble as well. How tyrannical, for example, the perpetual thought that my life might not be happy enough, so that I find myself coming to see my life in terms of lack, as something that does not live up to the stringent standards set by the champions of happiness who smile out in soft-focus from the back covers of books in the self-help department of the bookstore.

And so, it seems to me that there can be found in the various contemporary debates about happiness two dominant, and opposed, schools of thought. Both factions are agreed that there is some kind of trouble with happiness, although they differ as to the nature of the trouble itself. The first faction is that of the champions of happiness. For these individuals, the trouble with happiness is simply that we don't have enough of it. What we want is to be happy, they say. Happiness is our birthright. More than this, we *deserve* happiness. Those who favour this view often see happiness as a personal achievement. It is, in a way, all very Protestant. Happiness is something that we win through hard and serious work; and if we are not happy, then in all likelihood we have simply not tried hard enough. The proponents of this view delight in inspirational tales of square-jawed, often American, heroes who suffer imprisonment and torture at the hand of inscrutable, often Oriental, enemies, but who manage by means of reflection on the wisdom of the ancient Stoics, or else on the insights of Buddhism, to overcome the misery of their conditions, and to be happy despite everything. The message seems to boil down to this: if you, with your pitifully unheroic little life, are not happy, whilst these paragons of flourishing are happy, then you just need to pull your finger out and take responsibility (you can get a head start by buying this book, or by signing up to this twelve-step programme...).

That is one faction. The other faction is made up of miserabilists and gloom-mongers, the kinds of people who carry around dog-eared Penguin editions of Schopenhauer to guard against the dangers of fleeting cheerfulness, who get a kick out of proclaiming that all earthly happiness is a waste of time, and who insist that those who purport to offer any practical thoughts or guidance when it comes to human happiness are either deluded or charlatans or both. Most philosophers are, when it comes down to it, inclined to this second view, to the extent that one might think miserabilism to be the *sine qua non* of the philosophical life. Philosophers or not, the gloom-mongers are profoundly suspicious of the champions of happiness. They point out that if self-help books really worked, then there would only ever need to be one, after which the writing of self-help books would be redundant. They remind us that — as the publishers secretly know — the self-help industry flourishes precisely because the wretched books don't work. So they pick holes in the language of happiness, and our fretting obsession with happiness, they point to the multiple misuses of the language of happiness as a way of avoiding the other things that matter, they insist on bringing up Mao and Stalin at every opportunity, and they hunker down in their gloomy philosophical corners pointing out everything that is bad in the world. Sometimes, if you catch them unawares, if the light is just right, you can catch them smirking just a little, as if there is something about all of this complaint and miserabilist contrarianism that makes them curiously... well, curiously *happy*.

For me, however, the trouble with happiness is neither one of these things nor the other. The trouble with happiness is not that there is something called happiness that we don't have enough of, and we are not doing the right kinds of things to attain. Nor is the trouble with happiness the fact that happiness is some kind of delusory shadow-play that is used to cover up the real injustices of the world. Instead, the trouble with happiness is simply this: that we assume that there is one thing that is called happiness, and that in elevating this one thing above all other things that matter, we end up with a skewed vision of the human life, a distorted view of what we might hope for, and of what matters.

The philosophers are all very well; but when I think about happiness these days, I often find myself recalling the happiest man alive, over there in Aston, with his rum and his biscuits. And when I think back to that curious interview on the subject of happiness, it occurs to me now that one of the troubles with happiness is this: that in the heat of our debates, in the earnest intensity of our attempts to master happiness, we find ourselves unable to crack open a bottle of rum, sit back in our chairs and say, —Now *that*... that is a very *stupid* question.

And then to laugh until there are tears forming in the corners of our eyes.

Communes Revisited

Andrew Rigby

In this piece I want to look back to the late 1960s/early 1970s when I was a doctoral research student at Birmingham University studying the contemporary commune movement in the UK. If utopia is a 'no-where' place and time, then certain features of my life at that time viewed from today's vantage point certainly seem 'utopic' — only imaginable in some far-away never-never land.

I was a grammar school boy from a respectable working class background. I was brought up to see education as the means to social mobility (and respectability). So I did my homework, passed my exams and eventually discovered the wonderfully liberating world of university. I decided this was where I wanted to be — so I studied some more, passed some more exams, got a scholarship to do an MA at Essex University, then another scholarship to study for a PhD at Birmingham. But having got my scholarship award, what was I to research?

I remember I was on a vigil outside a company that was supplying the US military with equipment for use in Vietnam. To while away the long night, one of the other protesters started telling me about some kind of workers cooperative influenced by the utopian socialist ideas of Robert Owen. I began to read up about the utopian socialist tradition. I remember that Martin Buber's *Paths in Utopia* had a powerful impact on me, especially his characterisation of those 'utopians' who believed in the continuity between means and ends. For Buber the utopian socialist was one who believes 'that we must create here and now the space *now* possible for the thing for which we are striving, so that it may come to fulfilment *then*; he does not believe in the post-revolutionary leap, but he does believe in a continuity within which revolution is only the accomplishment, the setting free and extension of reality that has already grown to its true possibilities.'[1] Later I came across the writings of the German anarchist Gustav Landauer and his observation, which is still pinned up on my office wall as I type today: 'The state is a condition, a certain relationship between human beings, a mode of human behaviour, we destroy it by contracting other relationships, by behaving differently.'

Here was a tradition of thought and practice that sought to transform the world by nonviolent and non-coercive means, by the power of example and a constructive form of direct action. Here was my research topic — a study of those whom I believed were the contemporary carriers (in the 1960s) of that tradition, the communes and communards within the UK.

The commune movement was a part of a wider social and cultural movement with which I identified and which embraced various 'alternative' initiatives. In Birmingham there was the Handsworth Free School, the Birmingham Arts Lab, and the Free University of Birmingham. There was the music scene, the alternative press, the food co-ops, and the urban communes, as well as those groups planning to move out of the city to establish rural communes. Like other places in Britain and elsewhere during this period, the city had its own 'alternative' movement with which significant sections of, primarily, educated middle class youth identified to a greater or lesser extent. This was a movement associated with style — style as in fashion, but also style as in *lifestyle*, the notion that how you lived everyday life and related to others was the most significant dimension of any revolutionary project to save the world.

I feel so self-conscious now, as I reflect back on that time, but it was a period of messianic hopes. We really did

[1] M. Buber, *Paths in Utopia*, London: Routledge & Kegan Paul, 1949, p. 13.

believe that we could remake the world anew, and build Blake's New Jerusalem. And it seemed to me (and others) that at the forefront of this movement were the communes and the commune-dwellers. They were not just weekend drop-outs, they were living the revolution! They were not just talking (or writing) about it, they were doing it! They were the cells of the new world, exemplars of an alternative way of living which, along with all the other alternative institutions, would wean folk away from the old corrupt patterns so that the old world would eventually collapse in on itself for lack of support.

Throughout the late '60s and early '70s I travelled round visiting as many communes as I could. In 1971 the annual *Directory of Communes* listed some forty ventures, but I think a more accurate estimate of the number of self-defined communes or intentional communities in Britain at that time was nearer one hundred. It was a heterogeneous scene. I recall the stereotypical dope-heads talking about *vibrations* and the mystical union with the universe to be attained through acid. Damaged people also come to mind, lonely souls searching for some kind of sanctuary that would shield them from the harsh straight world. I still recall my shock on seeing a young man in one urban commune injecting himself with what I presumed was heroin. There were also the politicos, the anarchists and the pacifists, who had arrived at communes via the peace movement and various forms of community action, and who sought to live out their protest rather than just demonstrate on the streets at weekends. And then there were the professionals — social workers, teachers and the like — who were committed to their careers but sought alternative living arrangements to what many saw as the isolation and irrationality of semi-detached suburbia.

Looking back it seems like a completely 'other-world', and it was. It was a particular and peculiar epoch — when swathes of us had been radicalised by the Vietnam War at a time when issues like finding a job and a career and the threat of unemployment and destitution seemed very distant. There was that sense of freedom — that the world was there for reshaping.

Throughout the harsher decades since that time it has been all too easy to dismiss communes, communards and the wider alternative society/counter-cultural movement of the late 1960s as little more than the empty symbolic posturing of disaffected but relatively privileged middle class youth.

OK, maybe in emphasising the revolutionary significance of lifestyle we attributed too much importance to a movement that for many was merely a movement of fashion, rather than a sustained attempt to transform the very roots of domination and exploitation in our society.

And yes, maybe the challenge to the work ethic that was an integral part of the counter-culture was little more than a celebration of idleness by those whose age and communal lifestyle allowed them to escape the exigencies of earning a living, albeit temporarily.

And on reflection it is clear that there was a strong element of cultural elitism about the movement, a failure to engage with the concerns of everyday working people. When one believed that consciousness was the critical variable, it was too easy to slip into believing that domination and exploitation could be transcended merely by thinking differently.

There was an unhealthy narcissism in much of the focus upon the significance of the self, and a consequent exclusion of any concern with wider issues. In practice, the elevation of *doing your own thing* into a prime value resulted in people becoming victim to every passing whim and failing to respect the rights of others — a discrepancy between rhetoric and practice which was particularly marked in relation to the treatment of women within the institutions of the alternative society.

But even so, despite all these negative attributes, it was much more than this. It was a wonderful time when, in a way that it is hard to imagine now, considerable numbers of people enjoyed the space and the opportunity to experiment with their lives. It was a time of enormous creativity which stemmed from the utopian confidence that anything was possible. Moreover, it was during this period that the conception of struggle was deepened beyond a concern with class to embrace issues of identity and patterns of domination in all spheres of life.

However hedonistic and self-centred the period and the movement might appear when viewed in retrospect, most of those involved in communes and the wider alternative society movement of that time saw no disjunction between the process of transforming their own lives and the wider project of changing the world.

I have to confess that I still believe that this message is as relevant today as it was half a century ago.

My Grandmother's Kitchen, at Half Past Two on a Weekday Afternoon

Ian Clayton

My grandmother is iron, my grandfather is coal, and together they are golden.

My grandmother is a nurse to grazed knees, a fetcher and a carrier and she can fashion a meal from a dish clout. My grandfather stands over six feet, he once squeezed his raw bones into an eighteen inch seam, his body is covered in flecks of deep blue where the skin has grown over cuts. Now he is a tail gate ripper and he breathes in dust, that one day will take his breath.

My grandmother shells peas, kneads bread, skins rabbits and peels potatoes with a knife that once belonged to her mother. She rolls cotton and passes it through moist lips to thread through the smallest of eyes, sometimes without looking. She purls and knits her brows to fashion jumpers from patterns that she keeps in a table drawer. My grandmother pinches Woodbines from my grandfather's packet when he sleeps. She sews them into the shoulder seams of her frock.

It's nearly half past two. My grandfather is walking up the lane from the pit. My grandmother walks to the street corner and checks that he's on his way. She comes back to her kitchen and stirs the gravy. She places knives and forks, salt and pepper and a warm plate onto the wooden table.

My grandfather peeps his head around the back door and says what he always says, "Is it ready?" He takes off his cap and a gabardine coat and hangs both on a peg behind the stairs door. "I'll be two minutes."

He goes across to the sink and turns on the cold tap. He catches water in a cup he has made from two hands, then throws it into his eyes three or four times. He then puts his mouth to the tap and lets the water run across his lips. Next he fills his mouth with water and holds his head back full tilt. He gargles. He spits a mixture of black dust and phlegm into the white pot. The mixture is swallowed down the plug hole like an oyster down a throat.

He turns just as my grandmother has spooned gravy over his mashed potato and Yorkshire pudding. He holds her to him and leans to nuzzle her cheek. He sits to eat. He eats like a shark. He chews his meat, the muscle in his cheeks moving up and down in rhythm. When he's finished all of the food, he takes up his knife and with the blade starts to scrape up every last streak of gravy. He dabs his mouth with a clean white hankie and then leans back in his chair. "Bloody lovely that!"

My grandfather then turns on the wireless. He picks up the *Daily Mirror* and turns it to the racing page. He starts to mark off winners with a little stubby pencil that he likes to lick. After this he announces, "I'll have an hour." He lies on the sofa, his long legs curled into his body. My grandmother places an overcoat over him and tucks it down between the cushions and the base.

At half past four this morning my grandmother had stirred my grandfather. She had gone downstairs and fried sheep's brains for his breakfast. At the doorstep at quarter past five she had kissed him and felt the outside of his coat pocket. She had reassured herself that his lucky fossil was there. My grandfather carries in his work clothes a stone that once was a frog. He found it amongst the coal. The stone that millions of years ago was a frog is now a talisman, a lucky charm. One day when he forgot to take it to the pit, a rock fell from the roof and hit him on the side of his face.

My grandmother washes the pots. Then sits down and unpicks the seam on her frock, she slides out a Woodbine and sits on a little three-legged stool by the back door to blow smoke rings into a yard full of spotless clean washing flapping on a line.

She stubs out her Woodbine on the bottom of her shoe and throws the tab into the bin. She comes into the house and picks up a copy of the *Red Star* woman's magazine. My grandfather snores gently, his face the colour of rust, like a wash leather hanging on a fence to dry. His whiskers are like filings growing to make a five o'clock shadow. My grandmother reads romantic stories.

Utopias of the Nineteenth Century

Marie Louise Berneri

The history of Utopias in the nineteenth century is closely linked with the creation of the socialist movement, and it is sometimes difficult to distinguish between schemes which belong to the realm of Utopian thought and those which come within the province of practical social reform. There is hardly a single work dealing with social problems, published during this period, which has not, at some time or other, been described as Utopian. The word itself lost its original significance, and came to mean the opposite of scientific; "Utopian" became almost a term of abuse which self-styled scientific socialists were fond of hurling at their opponents. It is thanks to these Marxist judges that the list of nineteenth century Utopias has assumed such enormous proportions.

In *Socialism, Utopian and Scientific,* Frederick Engels gave a Marxist definition of the word "Utopian" which has come to be widely accepted. While until then a Utopia was considered as an imaginary ideal commonwealth whose realisation was impossible or difficult, Engels gave it a much wider meaning and included all social schemes which did not recognise the division of society into classes, the inevitability of the class struggle and of the social revolution. He classified [Henrick] Saint-Simon, [Charles] Fourier and [Robert] Owen among the Utopians, for "not one of them appears as a representative of the interests of the proletariat, which historical development had, in the meantime, produced. Like the French philosophers, they do not claim to emancipate a particular class to begin with, but all humanity at once."

Engels, furthermore, reproached "Utopian" writers for not having understood that socialism would be possible only when the capitalist regime had achieved a certain degree of development: "To the crude conditions of capitalistic production and the crude class conditions corresponded crude theories. The solution of the social problems, which as yet lay hidden in undeveloped economic conditions, the Utopians attempted to evolve out of the human brain. Society presented nothing but wrongs; to remove these was the task of reason. It was necessary, then, to discover a new and more perfect social order and to impose this upon society from without by propaganda, and, whenever it was possible, by the example of model experiments. These new social systems were foredoomed as Utopian; the more completely they were worked out in detail, the more they could not avoid drifting off into 'pure fantasies'."

Engels' description of socialist Utopias is substantially correct. Most of them want all the means of production and distribution to be held in common, but do not think that a revolution is necessary to bring this about. They assume that the State can take over the economic machinery of a country in a peaceful manner, when the majority of the population have agreed that it is the most sensible solution. They do not think that there is an irreducible antagonism between classes, and that the proletariat is the only class able to achieve a revolution. Again, in contradiction to Marxist theories, they assert that a new society can be created at any time or place, provided governments and peoples are resolved to bring it into being; they see no relation between the development of capitalism and the possibility of creating a new society.

Engels was not, however, justified in assuming that the "Utopian" schemes were less realistic than those of the "scientific" socialists. In the light of the history of the past century it would be a difficult task to decide which school of socialism deserves the description of "Utopian". The high development of capitalism, far from bringing nearer the day of the revolution, has created a new class of technicians and managers, highly paid workers and trade union leaders whose interests are identified with those of the capitalist class. The only two European countries which have, during the past thirty years,* attempted to carry out social revolutions, Russia and Spain, were countries where capitalism had not yet reached a high degree of development. We have seen, furthermore, that state socialism has been partially realised in several countries, not by the militant action of the working class, but by governments holding power through an elected Parliament. More paradoxical still, from a Marxist viewpoint, fascist governments have been obliged to adopt measures of social reform similar to those advocated by socialists.

Socialism, as we know it today, is nearer to the conceptions of the "Utopian" socialists than to those of Karl Marx, the founder of scientific socialism. It no longer recognises the inevitability of the class struggle, and aims at gradual social reforms which will eventually eliminate the economic differences between capitalists and workers. Even in a country like Russia, which claims to have carried out a Marxist revolution, the structure of society resembles more closely that described by some Utopian writers than that foreseen by Marx or Lenin. It might be wiser, therefore, to leave aside what seems today an arbitrary division between Utopian and scientific socialists, and to consider only the most representative of those works which remain in the Utopian tradition by describing ideal commonwealths in some imaginary country or in an imaginary future.

At the time of the Renaissance, Utopian thought had received a strong impetus from the new philosophical ideas, the birth of national states and the discovery of the

---

*Berneri was writing in the 1940s.

New World. At the beginning of the nineteenth century events of similar magnitude infused it with new life: these included the after-effects of the French Revolution, the rapid development of industry and the elaboration of socialist systems. The French Revolution had given power to the bourgeoisie, but at the same time it had asserted the rights of the workers and peasants, who had shown their readiness to defend them by force. The victorious bourgeoisie could not shut its eyes to social inequalities which might at any moment release a strong revolutionary movement. A few humanitarian thinkers and philanthropists tried to alleviate the growing misery of the people, and some went so far as to demand that equality which had been preached by pre-revolutionary philosophers and which was one of the supposed aims of the Revolution. But they did not trust the people, whom they feared could only change the system by revolutionary methods, and they sought a pacific solution through social reform. As Kropotkin pointed out in his introduction to *The Conquest of Bread,** "...writing during the period of reaction which had followed the French Revolution, and seeing more its failures than its successes, they did not trust the masses, and they did not appeal to them for bringing about the changes which they thought necessary. They put their faith, on the contrary, in some great ruler, some Socialist Napoleon. He would understand the new revelation; he would be convinced of its desirability by the successful experiment of the phalansteries, or associations; and he would peacefully accomplish by his own authority the revolution which would bring well-being and happiness to mankind. A military genius, Napoleon, had just been ruling Europe; why should not a social genius come forward, carry Europe with him and translate the new Gospel into life?"

---

*Republished in 2008 by AK Press.

The industrial revolution had opened new horizons, and it seemed to many that it offered a solution to poverty and inequality. There were apparently no limits to the increase of production, and therefore there seemed no reason why everyone should not live like a bourgeois. Equality would not entail a sacrifice for anybody, since the new society would not decrease the comfort of the rich, but raise that of the poor to their level. While Utopias in the past had stressed the need for detachment from material goods, those of the nineteenth century sought happiness in the satisfaction of an ever-increasing number of material needs. It was not only that industrial progress now allowed greater luxury; the whole attitude towards material pleasure was altered. In [Thomas] More's *Utopia* people led an austere life, not out of necessity, for they had gold and silver with which they could have bought goods from foreign countries and thereby improved their standard of living, but because they thought that luxury would inevitably bring corruption and moral degeneration. With a few exceptions such as Francis Bacon, Utopian writers had conceived progress in terms of mental, physical and moral improvement of men, and this could not be achieved if too much importance were given to material goods. A too-great indulgence of the flesh would bring corruption of the mind. We find no such moralistic preoccupations in nineteenth century Utopians; they were shamelessly materialistic and fell little short of calculating individual happiness in terms of pieces of furniture, articles of clothing or the number of courses served at each meal. Only occasionally do we find a reaction against this tendency, as in William Morris's *News from Nowhere.*

The influence of the "fathers of socialism" on the Utopias of the nineteenth century was, of course, considerable. Owen, Fourier and Saint-Simon not only influenced Utopias through their theoretical writings, but through their concrete plans of social reform and of "villages of cooperation," parallelograms or phalansteries, have inspired many features of later Utopias. In some respects, however, Owen and Fourier differ from the main trend of socialist thought of the nineteenth century, for they do not advocate a centralised government and an intensive industrialisation of the countryside but believe, on the contrary, in small autonomous agricultural communities. Owen gives the initiative of forming these small agricultural communes, not containing more than 3,000 inhabitants, to some enlightened government, but they must be self-supporting and run by autonomous administrations. All the internal affairs would be governed by a general Council, composed of all the members of the community between the ages of thirty and forty, while all the external affairs would be administered by another general council, composed of all the members from the ages of forty to sixty. All the members of the commune would be equal, and would receive an equal share of the goods produced; the general councils would rule according to the laws of human nature. When the whole world had become covered by federations of agricultural communities, governments would become unnecessary and would disappear altogether. Owen's ideas on education are those which perhaps had the greatest influence on Utopian writers. He repeatedly stated throughout his writings that "the character of man, is, without a single exception, always formed for him; that it may be, and is, chiefly, created by his predecessors; that they give him, or may give him, his ideas and habits, which are the powers that govern and direct his conduct." It was therefore the task of education to train men to "live without idleness, without poverty, without crime and without punishment." Owen's attempts to put his ideas into practice, first at New Lanark and later in the communities which he founded in America, inspired many similar experiments, and in the nineteenth century it is not infrequent to find that Utopias give birth to community movements.

The name of Fourier is often linked to that of Owen because of certain superficial resemblances between the two thinkers and in spite of the fact that Fourier always referred to Owen in the most disparaging terms. Fourier has been called, more unjustly than Owen, a "father of socialism," for he did not in fact believe in the community of goods. The idea was indeed wholly repellent to him, since he thought inequality indispensable to the smooth running of his ideal society. Though he favoured the abolition of wages, he thought that dividends should be paid according to the amount of capital invested, the results, and the talents of the individual shareholders. Fourier, however, believed that society should provide even for those who refused to work, not only to free work from its compulsory nature but because society has a duty towards its members whether they produce or not. But work was to be made so attractive and to provide so many enjoyable things that there would be very few idlers.

Fourier did not put his faith in any enlightened government, but he hoped to find some wealthy patron who would provide the necessary funds to set up a phalanstery, and that people would be so struck by its admirable results that identical phalansteries would soon cover the whole earth. The advantage of his system, he claimed, was to combine the interests of capitalists, workers and consumers by uniting all these functions in the same individual. These were ideas which were taken up by many associationists in the latter half of the nineteenth century, and even upheld by a section of the socialist movement of today. As Charles Gide remarks in *A History of Economic Doctrines:* "A programme which aims, not at the abolition of property, but at the extinction of the wage-earner by giving him the right of holding property on the joint-stock principle, which looks to succeed, not by advocating class war, but by fostering cooperation of capital with labour and managing ability, and attempts to reconcile the conflicting interests of capitalist and worker, of producer and consumer, debtor and creditor, by welding those interests together in one and the same person, is by no means commonplace. Such was the ideal of the French working classes until Marxian collectivism took its place, and it is quite possible that its deposition may be only temporary after all."

Charles Fourier's eccentricity prevented him from exercising a wide influence, but his writings contain such a wealth of ideas as to make them an inexhaustible source of inspiration for social reformers, and even his bitterest opponents were influenced by him. His anticipation of garden cities, which would replace the agglomeration of big cities, his advocacy of market gardening, which was to replace extensive agriculture, his study of the means by which work can be made attractive, and his teachings on education and sexual questions, only attracted the direct attention of a small minority, it is true, but through this medium they are known to many who have never read Fourier's writings.

Though Fourier himself was never able to realise his dream of setting up a phalanstery, communities based on his ideas were created both in France and in America. The most celebrated, although it did not last very long, was that of Brook Farm* in the United States. Associations of producers and consumers run according to Fourier's principles were also set up with a certain degree of success.

Among the "fathers of socialism" we should also mention Saint-Simon, for he, and perhaps even more his followers, put forward ideas which are to be found in many Utopias of the latter half of the nineteenth century. While Owen and Fourier, represented, in many respects, a reaction against industrialism by wanting a return to small agricultural communities, Saint-Simon was an enthusiastic supporter of the new industrial regime and of the new ruling class created by the Great Revolution and enriched by the rapid expansion of industry. Under the old order, society was ruled by nobles and priests.

---

*The subject of Hawthorne's novel, *The Blithedale Romance.*

These were now to be replaced by the bourgeoisie whose main task was to encourage the progress of science and industry. It would be ridiculous, said Saint-Simon, for an industrial society to be ruled by nobles who have no longer any *raison d'être,* or by politicians who know nothing of industrial problems. The old form of governments must disappear for they are completely useless to society. In the famous document which is known as *Saint-Simon's Parable* (published in 1832) he showed vividly that the vital section of society was composed of scientists, technicians, bankers and businessmen and not of politicians, state officials or priests.

"Let us suppose," he said, "that France suddenly loses fifty of her first-class doctors, fifty first-class chemists, fifty first-class physiologists, fifty first-class bankers, two hundred of her best merchants, six hundred of her foremost agriculturists, five hundred of her most capable ironmasters, etc. (enumerating the principal industries). Seeing that these men are its most indispensable producers, makers of its most important products, the minute that it loses these the nation will degenerate into a mere soulless body and fall into a state of despicable weakness in the eyes of rival nations, and will remain in this subordinate position so long as the loss remains and their places are vacant. Let us take another supposition. Imagine that France retains all her men of genius, whether in the arts and sciences or in the crafts and industries, but has the misfortune to lose on the same day the king's brother, the Duke of Angoulème, and all the other members of the royal family; all the great officers of the Crown; all ministers of State, whether at the head of a department or not; all the Privy Councillors; all the masters of requests; all the marshals, cardinals, archbishops, bishops, grand vicars and canons; all prefects and sub-prefects; all Government employees; all the judges; and on top of that a hundred thousand proprietors — the cream of her nobility. Such an overwhelming catastrophe would certainly aggrieve the French, for they are a kindly-disposed nation. But the loss of a hundred and thirty thousand of the best-reputed individuals in the State would give rise to sorrow of a purely sentimental kind. It would not cause the community the least inconvenience."*

Already in 1816 Saint-Simon had declared that politics is the science of production and that eventually it would be completely absorbed by economics; France was to be turned into a factory and the nation organised on the model of a vast workshop. In the new society all class distinctions would disappear; there would only be workers, the term being used in its larger sense to include manufacturers, scientists, bankers and artists. But this does not mean that all would be equal, since everyone would receive according to his capacities (and even according to the capital invested).

The originality of Saint-Simon consists in giving to the best industrial leaders, scientists, bankers, etc., the task of administering the country. In other words the old government of politicians will be replaced by a government of "managers." More than a hundred years before we began to talk of a managerial class or of a "managerial revolution," Saint-Simon had foreseen that the industrial revolution would give birth to a new ruling class. Edward Bellamy echoes Saint-Simon, while building his Utopia on a socialistic basis. The idea that the governing of men must be replaced by the administration of things, and that all the problems of society resolve themselves into that of production, became current during the nineteenth century. In one of the many schemes of government which he put forward, Saint-Simon gives the executive power to a Chamber of Deputies composed of representatives of commerce, industry, manufacture and agriculture, who would accept or reject the legislative proposals submitted to them by two Chambers composed of scientists, artists

---

*Quoted in *A History of Economic Doctrines* by C. Gide and C. Rist.

and engineers. The only task of this "government" would be to increase the material wealth of the country. This system left no initiative to the mass of the workers, in whom Saint-Simon had no faith whatever: "The problem of social organisation," he said, "must be solved for the people. The people themselves are passive and listless and must be discounted in any consideration of the question. The best way is to entrust public administration to the care of the industrial chiefs, who will always directly attempt to give the widest possible scope to their undertakings, with the result that their efforts in this direction will lead to the maximum expansion of the amount of work executed by the mass of the people." Though socialist thinkers professed to be shocked by Saint-Simon's high-handed way of dealing with the "proletariat", the idea that the administration of a country is a matter for experts, and that the state machine is to be composed of committees or commissariats of technicians and industrial chiefs is to be found in many socialist writings, and in Russia we have seen the creation of a managerial class endowed, as Saint-Simon would have advocated, with economic and political privileges, though he would have strongly disapproved of the retention of a political party and professional politicians.

While Owen, Fourier and Saint-Simon put little reliance on the intervention of the State to transform the structure of society, Louis Blanc is one of the first socialists to give the State the task of reforming society. He asserted that it was the duty of the State to see that the "right to work" should be respected and thereby abolish crimes, which are all due to poverty. Only by eliminating competition can the government abolish unemployment, poverty and the moral degradation which result from them. Its task is therefore to become "the supreme regulator of production" and, to begin with, it must set up "social workshops" in the most important branches of industry, and gradually expand them to the whole country. The State would eventually become the sole owner of all the means of production, at least so long as inequalities exist, for when perfect equality reigned the State would wither away.

Louis Blanc's proposals of reform were expounded in a booklet entitled *L'Organisation du Travail,* published in 1839, which enjoyed an immense popularity at the time. It is often described as a Utopia, though it is just the opposite, being a proposal of immediate reform, and the beginning of the institution of a collectivist system of production. That Louis Blanc himself strongly believed in the practicability of his proposals is shown by the fact that, after the 1848 Revolution, he asked the General Assembly to set up a Ministry of Progress which would carry out the plan he had outlined in *L'Organisation du Travail.* The Ministry of Progress would "set the revolution in movement": banks, railways and mines would be nationalised, and the money would be used to set up social workshops in the most important branches of industry. The State would appoint officials who would direct the factory for the first year, but once the workers would have come to know one another and take an interest in the enterprise, they would elect their own officials. Each member of the social workshop would have the right to dispose of the produce of his labour as he thought fit, but soon "the obvious economy and unquestionable excellence of community life would lead from the association of work to the voluntary association for the satisfaction of needs and pleasures." Louis Blanc also put forward a plan for the collective cultivation of the land by the creation of agricultural social workshops run upon similar principles to those of the industrial social workshops. Louis Blanc's scheme was never put into practice. The attempt to set up National Workshops in 1848 was only made by the government in order to discredit his ideas, but many productive cooperative societies arose in France at that time under the influence of his writings. The Utopias of the nineteenth century which derive their inspiration from the theories which we have briefly considered are on the whole depressingly uninspiring. They aim at setting up a vast machinery which will ensure a perfect running of society and bring material wellbeing to everyone. But in these intricate mechanisms man's individuality is completely lost. The State becomes an all-wise, all-providing God which can never make any mistakes — and if it did no one would have the power to correct them. Whether State Socialism is administered through universal suffrage, as in Cabet's *Voyage to Icaria,* or through an industrial hierarchy as in Bellamy's *Looking Backward,* the results are the same: man is unable to express his personality except through the channels provided by the State. He becomes an automaton, working the number of hours prescribed by law, fulfilling tasks which excessive industrialisation has rendered monotonous and impersonal. The produce of his labour is accumulated in gigantic storehouses, to be consumed by a community with which he has no real links, for it is too enormous and centralised to allow intimate relations. An attempt is sometimes made to create a sense of community by uniting all the people of the same district in communal restaurants, for example, but, like so many other institutions of the nineteenth century Utopias, it is a purely artificial means of creating a community spirit. In Utopias of the past such as Andreae's *Christianopolis* the unity of the community was a "functional" one. Workers engaged in the same craft met to discuss the problems related to their work, the whole community assembled to discuss the quantity of food, clothing, furniture, etc, which they needed, and production was regulated according to the needs of a community which, because of its small size, they knew intimately. But in the Utopias of the nineteenth century the amount of autonomy granted to factory committees or consumers' unions is mostly fictitious. There is little which the workers can discuss when everything is regulated by the State, thanks to its experts and bureaux of statistics. As [Lewis] Mumford has pointed out, "These Utopias become vast reticulations of steel and red-tape, until we feel that we are caught in the Nightmare of the Age of Machinery, and shall never escape... the means has become the end, and the genuine problem of ends has been forgotten... I doubt whether an intelligent peasant in India or China would get out of the whole batch of these Utopias a single idea which would have any bearing on the life he has experienced — so little of human significance remains when the problems of mechanical and political organisation have been disposed of!"

There are fortunately a few Utopias where man comes into his own again, where he is not reduced to a machine which has to be fed, clothed and housed just like any piece of machinery that requires careful handling if it is to give the maximum output, where he is not moulded from his youth into a "good citizen," that is to say, a citizen perfectly obedient to the law and incapable of thinking for himself. Of these Utopias of free socialism William Morris's *News from Nowhere* is the most attractive, and has a permanent quality which allows it to be still widely read in this country as well as abroad. There are also a number of Utopian romances such as W.H. Hudson's *The Crystal Age* and W.H. Mallock's *The New Republic,* which make no pretence of giving a fool-proof plan for a perfect society, but which describe the type of community in which the authors would like to live. These romances, as W.H. Hudson himself has pointed out, "however fantastic they may be, have for most of us a perennial mild interest since they are born of a common feeling — a sense of dissatisfaction" with the existing order of things, combined with a vague faith in or hope of a better one to come... (One cannot) help asking one another, What is your dream, your ideal? What is your News from Nowhere? However little one may feel attracted towards Hudson's sexless society, or W.H. Mallock's refined "country house," one cannot help finding these Utopian writers somewhat refreshing after the numberless Messiahs with whom the path of the nineteenth century is strewn.

I would have liked to include in this section extracts from Butler's *Erewhon,* for it satirises many ideas frequently expressed in the Utopias of the nineteenth century, and in particular the belief that the extensive use of machinery will automatically bring happiness to mankind, but *Erewhon* cannot properly be considered as a Utopia. It belongs, as Desmond MacCarthy has remarked, "to the same class of fiction as *Gulliver's Travels;* those books in which an imaginary civilisation is used as a device for criticising our own." I have included instead, in the book from which this article is taken, extracts from Eugene Richter's *Pictures of a Socialistic Future,* a satirical Utopia which has no philosophical pretensions, but illustrates many objections which the Utopias of state-socialism arouse in one's mind.

There are few Utopias of the nineteenth century which can be read today without a feeling of utter boredom, unless they succeed in amusing us by the obvious conceit of their authors in thinking themselves the saviours of mankind. The Utopias of the Renaissance contained many unattractive features, yet they had a breadth of vision which commanded respect; those of the seventeenth century presented many extravagant ideas, yet they revealed searching, dissatisfied minds with which one sympathises; but, though we are in many ways familiar with the thought of the Utopias of the nineteenth century, they are nevertheless more foreign to us than those of a more distant past. In spite of the fact that these Utopian writers were no doubt inspired by the highest motives, on cannot help "feeling bitter about the nineteenth century", like the old man in *News from Nowhere,* bitter even about the love these utopian writers lavish on humanity, for they seem like so many over-affectionate and over-anxious mothers who would kill their sons with attention and kindness rather than let them enjoy one moment of freedom.

Dreaming London
The Future City in William Morris and Others
Peter Preston

During the time I was working on this essay, I spent a couple of nights at a riverside hotel in Richmond-on-Thames. Wakeful at dawn, I stood looking out of the window. A garden sloped down to the river; on one side stood a mighty horse chestnut tree, on the other a London plane towered above the rooftops. Occasional joggers passed on the towpath and scullers glided in both directions. From my left the river flowed down from its source in Gloucestershire, past Kelmscott Manor, through Oxfordshire and Berkshire. To my right it continued its eastward course past Hammersmith and Kelmscott House, through the centre of London and eventually to the sea. Across the river lay an extensive area of housing, some late nineteenth-century, some recent, built in a muted and curiously box-like classical style: huge square blocks of exclusive apartments and town houses. On the other side of the hotel lay the centre of Richmond, which retains its old street layout, crammed with familiar chain stores, as well as designer shops and chic restaurants: all the marks of contemporary retail culture, in an eighteenth- and nineteenth-century village context. Looking across the river it took no great effort of the imagination to make the modern houses and shops disappear and replace them with an older Richmond, a Richmond of cottages, small shops, farms, fields and trees, with the river as its main highway. It took no great effort, in other words, to find myself dreaming London.

William Morris, of course, also dismissed a modern version of London and replaced it with a dream city:

Forget the spreading of the hideous town;
Think rather of the pack-horse on the down,
And dream of London, small, and white, and clean,
The clear Thames bordered by its gardens green ...[1]

These familiar lines from the "Prologue" to *The Earthly Paradise* (1868–70) are an injunction to readers to exercise their imagination and enter Morris's vision of a late fourteenth-century London, Chaucer's bright compact city, rich with foreign goods, and shorn of its polluting industrial activity. Twenty years later, Morris created another London dreamer, his alter ego in William Guest, the narrator *of News from Nowhere* (1890). Depressed by the sectarian squabbles "up at the League",[2] he falls into a restless sleep, and wakes to find that the dirty, crowded city of the 1880s and 1890s has disappeared and has been replaced by a London that resembles the city in the dream that opens *The Earthly Paradise.*

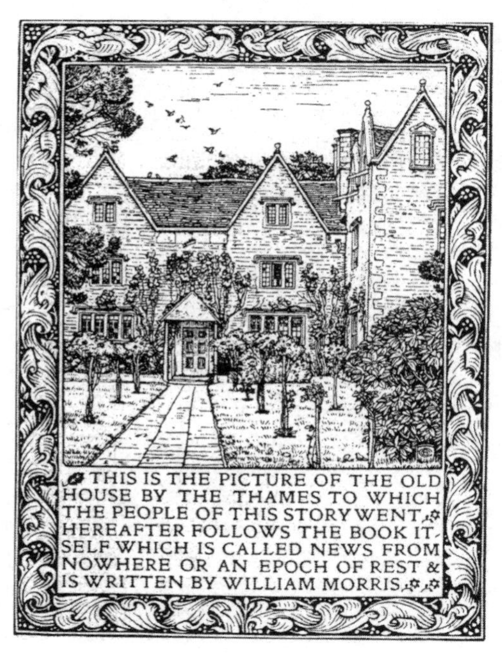

Those familiar with Morris's life and career are accustomed to regard *News from Nowhere* as a centrepiece in Morris's complex social and artistic vision, with dimensions drawn from the past, applied to the present and linked in hope to the future. The text is a meeting-place for Morris's ideas and preoccupations concerning history, politics, economics, social organisation, gender relations, art and labour. It addresses issues of desire and necessity, and is charged with both passionate hope and regretful acceptance. Its fluvial structure, following the bends of the river towards the unnamed house that is Kelmscott Manor, embodies a journey into both a social future and Morris's personal past. Belonging to the final phase of Morris's long career, *News from Nowhere* seems to present itself as a summation of Morris's achievements and ideals.

This essay places *News from Nowhere* within a mode of imaginative writing about London. It reads Morris's text in relation to works by other London dreamers, other visionaries of a future city, reaching back to the late eighteenth century, through the nineteenth century and into the early years of the twentieth. By locating Morris within this strand of London writing, I am not suggesting that Morris thought of himself within this literary tradition, although it is clear that Morris was aware that *News from Nowhere* belonged with a body of English Utopian writing; its immediate occasion was Morris's reaction to Edward Bellamy's *Looking Backward* (1888).[3] Nor am I suggesting that he was aware of the work of all or any of the writers I shall discuss, just as he could not have foreseen the directions taken by his successors. Nonetheless, Morris contributes to a body of prophetic and speculative writing about the future of the city, and in doing so not only reshapes the ways in which we might read his predecessors and contemporaries, but helps to determine the ways in which those who succeeded him might dream about the future city.

II

In 1774, Horace Walpole, who had drawn freely from the past to transform Strawberry Hill into a Gothic extravaganza, permitted himself a glimpse into the future. "The next Augustan age", he wrote to Sir Horace Mann, "will dawn on the other side of the Atlantic. There will perhaps be a Thucydides at Boston, a Xenophon at New York, and in time a Virgil at Mexico and a Newton at Peru. At last some curious traveller from Lima will visit England and give a description of the ruins of St Paul's."[4] Walpole, like many privileged young men of his time, had made the Grand Tour, and had seen the melancholy remains of once-great empires, so the analogy of a tourist from the New World viewing the ruins of London's most prominent classical building came naturally to him; and his belief in the historical inevitability of decline and decay was shared by other writers. Sir Richard Phillips, writing in *The Monthly Magazine* in 1811, offered a nightmare vision of London's future:

> ...great cities contain in their very greatness, the seeds of premature and rapid decay. London will increase, as long as certain causes operate which she cannot control ... these failing, the houses will become too numerous for the inhabitants, and certain districts will be occupied by beggary and vice, or become depopulated. The disease will spread... and ruin will follow ruin till the entire city is disgusting to the remnant of the inhabitants. Such have been the causes of the decay of all overgrown cities. Nineveh, Babylon, Antioch, and Thebes... Rome, Delhi and Alexandria are partaking the same inevitable fate, and London must some time... succumb under the destiny of everything human.[5]

In the following year, Anna Laetitia Barbauld published *Eighteen Hundred and Eleven, A Poem* (1812), in which she similarly evokes a great city that is doomed to fade, for "fairest flowers bloom but to decay;/The worm in thy core, thy glories pass away."

Inevitably, the tourists come to St Paul's, one of "the hallowed mansions of the silent dead/... the long isle and vaulted dome/Where Genius and Valour find a home" and "Where all above is still, as all beneath." From this future London, haunted by crime and want, the spirit of art and civilisation flees, and settles instead in the New World, "On Andes' heights .../On Chimborazo's summits", to "[pour] through feeble souls a higher life" and cry "Thy world, Columbus, shall be free."[6]

The pessimism of Barbauld's poem, with its foreshadowing of London's social and economic decline, is characteristic of the early decades of the nineteenth century, as is its accompanying assumption of a shift in the cultural centre of gravity to continents distant from Europe. In his sprightly "Dedication" to *Peter Bell the Third* (1819), Shelley imagines a similar fate for London's landmarks, "when St Paul's and Westminster Abbey shall stand, shapeless and nameless ruins, in the midst of an unpeopled marsh; when the piers of Waterloo Bridge shall become the nuclei of islets of reeds and osiers, and cast the jagged shadows of the broken arches on the solitary stream." He goes on to speculate that by this time "some transatlantic commentator" will be weighing poetry "in the scales of some new and now unimagined system of criticism."[7] And in the Victorian period, William Thackeray picks up, in a characteristically humorous yet melancholy tone, if not the anticipation of cultural realignment, then of desertion and a reduction in status from a city of power to a city of antiquity. In *Vanity Fair* (1847–48) he writes "some day or other (but it will be after our time, thank goodness), Hyde Park will be no better known than the celebrated horticultural outskirts of Babylon, and Belgrave Square will be as desolate as Baker Street, or Tadmor in the wilderness."[8]

However, the most definitive and enduring image of a future visitor from a distant land surveying a devastated London was created in 1840, by the historian

Thomas Macaulay. Reviewing Ranke's *History of the Popes of Rome,* Macaulay commented on the longevity of the Catholic Church: "... she may still exist in undiminished vigour when some traveller from New Zealand shall, in the midst of a vast solitude, take his stand on a broken arch of London Bridge to sketch the ruins of St Paul's."[9] The extent to which this passage made its way into the city discourse of the remainder of the nineteenth century is extraordinary. The *Edinburgh Review* was a prestigious journal and its views in the literary sphere were influential. In 1840 Macaulay had been a star of the *Edinburgh Review* for fifteen years, and had recently returned from a spell as an administrator in British India. His *Essays Critical and Historical,* published in 1843, and including the Ranke review, was one of the best sellers of the nineteenth century. It is therefore perhaps unsurprising that Macaulay's antipodean artist should have gained such a hold on the imagination of other writers.

The journalist George Augustus Sala, for instance, invokes Macaulay's image in one of the topographical essays of *Twice Round the Clock,* published in 1858: "Foremost among names familiar to British mouths is Covent Garden. The provincial knows it; the American knows it; Lord Macaulay's New Zealander will come to meditate among the moss-grown arcades, when he makes that celebrated sketching excursion we have so long been promised."[10] In her novel *Aurora Floyd* (1862–63), Mary Elizabeth Braddon comments on a celebrated confectioner's shop: "When poor Thomas Babington Macaulay's New Zealander shall come to ponder over the ruins of St Paul's, he will visit the remains of the humbler temple in Berkeley Square, and wonder at the ice-pails and jelly-moulds, the refrigerators and stewpans, the hot plates long cold and unheeded, and all the mysterious paraphernalia of the dead art."[11] A year later, the American writer Nathaniel Hawthorne remarks of the Thames Tunnel that it "has turned out a sublime piece of folly;

and when the New Zealander of distant ages shall have moralised sufficiently among the ruins of London Bridge, he will bethink himself that somewhere thereabouts was the marvellous Tunnel, the very existence of which will seem to him as incredible as that of the hanging gardens of Babylon."[12] In the domestic sphere, Charles Dickens, describing preparations for theatrical performances at his house in 1856, wrote that "[t]he theatre partition is put up, and is a work of such terrific solidity that I suppose it will be dug up, ages hence, from the ruins of London, by that Australian of Macaulay's who is to be impressed by its ashes."[13] Macaulay's artist may have shifted countries in Dickens's imperfect recollection, but that does not detract from his use of the allusion.

A telling version of the New Zealander can be found in Blanchard Jerrold and Gustave Doré's *London: a Pilgrimage,* published in 1872. Doré was well-known as an illustrator of Dante, the Bible and Tennyson.[14] His engravings of contemporary London were executed in 1869–71, and Jerrold was a professional writer employed to provide a commentary on Doré's images. The resulting book is more valuable for its visual than its literary qualities, since Jerrold has little to offer that can match the power of Doré's engravings. The New Zealander appears towards the end of the volume, accompanied by Jerrold's attempt at a peroration:

> Now we have watched the fleets into noisy Billingsgate and now gossiped looking towards Wren's grand dome, shaping Macaulay's dream of the far future, with the tourist New Zealander upon the broken parapets contemplating something matching
>
> "The glory that was Greece
> The grandeur that was Rome."[15]

With its incorporation of Edgar Allan Poe's lines, the sentiment is familiar enough, and returns to that well-established idea of the fate of empires.[16] It illustrates, however, the continuing influence of Macaulay's words.

Perhaps the most remarkable example of this influence, however, and the most elaborated development of Macaulay's New Zealander trope, can be found in the work of Anthony Trollope, and it is an example no less remarkable for having been unpublished at the time of its composition and unknown, except to Trollope scholars, for nearly a century after the author's death. *The New Zealander* was first written in 1855–56, but remained unpublished until 1972.[17] It has nothing to do with New Zealand: although Trollope was rare among his contemporaries in visiting that country, he did not travel there until 1871–72. His New Zealander is Macaulay's, the future sketcher of ancient ruins, although Trollope adds to Macaulay's version a few dramatic details of his own, describing "some ornate man of art, some future polished tourist, standing on the ruins of London Bridge, while he sketch(es) the time-worn columns and shattered though standing dome of our St Paul's" (4). Trollope's characterisation of the tourist as "ornate" and "polished" emphasises London's future role as the destination rather than the starting-point of a reconfigured Grand Tour; "time-worn" and "shattered though standing" suggest a kind of weary heroism in the ruins; while the possessive pronoun "our" hints at the collapse of a shared heritage. But what distinguishes Trollope's use of the New Zealander is that he does not consign his visit to the distant future. "Is the time quickly coming," the book begins, "when the New Zealander shall supplant the Englishman in the history of the civilisation of the world? Have the glories of Great Britain reached their climax, culminated, and begun to pale?" This idea of a present rather than a future decline is what animates *The New Zealander,* and gives it point and force. Trollope's reflections on the centres of power such as the Crown, Parliament, the Church, the Law, the Civil Service and the Press all located in the capital not only accept the concept of decadence as "the inheritance we have received from Adam" (60), but also suggest that the end point of that decadence may be closer than his potential readers believe.[18] London's large, solid buildings, the material symbols of Britain's power and influence, maybe an illusion, and Trollope asks his readers the challenging question "Is the Zealander already coming to feed his pride with our fall?" (10).

The New Zealander therefore functions within Trollope's text as both a monitory and an admonitory figure. For, unlike other writers who take up Macaulay's metaphor, Trollope does not maintain the presence of the New Zealander at a safe distance, engaged in philosophical contemplation or the gentlemanly pursuit of sketching. Trollope's New Zealander, with his potential to be not merely a tourist but an invader, represents a threat; a benevolent one to be sure, but carrying sufficient force to bring him to the heart of London's sites of power. In the House of Commons, for example, any member inclined to vote that black is white "does whatever lies in him to destroy the honour of England and hasten the coming of the New Zealander." (130) The House of Lords, with its "worship of the dead, of things that are dead as well as men" may not contain sufficient strength "to exclude from London Bridge that gentleman from the Pacific, who is, we are told, to visit us in our decadence." (141) Trollope goes on to observe that while the prospect of a New Zealander on London Bridge may be "sufficiently trying to the nerves of an Englishman", he certainly does not want to see him, "even in our mind's eye, lolling in the House of Lords on the seat of our Queen; or wondering at the obsolete regalia of our past royalty." (142) Only at the end of his narrative does Trollope entertain the idea that it might be possible to postpone indefinitely the coming of the New Zealander. Only in his final chapter does he express the hope that his "enterprising polished friend" need not hurry to visit England (207). But to postpone this visit, will require an effort of perception and discrimination on the part of the English:

> ...It cannot be but that we shall learn to call dishonesty and want of truth by their proper names, and to know them when we meet them.
>
> Let us learn to do that, and we shall then do whatever in us lies to postpone the coming of the New Zealander (211).

III

In "The Modern Thames", an essay written in 1885,[19] Richard Jefferies remarked that "the red deer can never again drink at the Thames in the dusk of the evening while our civilisation endures"; in the same year, Jefferies published *After London; or, Wild England,* in which he foresaw the end of that civilisation. Morris read this "queer book" soon after it was published and wrote to Georgiana Burne-Jones: "I rather like it: absurd hopes curled round my heart as I read it. I rather wish I were thirty years younger. I want to see the game played out."[20] The game to which he refers is the reversion to barbarism described in Jefferies' novel, to which, as Norman Kelvin puts it, Morris gave "morbid but unqualified assent".[21] Morris articulates this assent in a later letter to Georgie.

> I have [no] more faith than a grain of mustard in the future history of "civilisation", which I *know* now is doomed to destruction, and probably before very long: what a joy it is to think of! And how often it consoles me to think of barbarism once more flooding the world, and real feelings and passions, however rudimentary, taking the place of our wretched hypocrisies. With this thought in my mind all the history of the past is lighted up and lives again to me. I used really to despair once because I thought that what the idiots of our day call progress would go on perfecting itself: happily, I know now that all that will have a sudden check — sudden in appearance I mean — "as it was in the days of Noë".[22]

Although Morris does not mention *After London* in his letter, it clearly lies behind what he writes. In particular, the "sudden check", the unexpected, apocalyptic catastrophe that destroys modern civilisation, suggests the disaster, never fully identified, that has led in Jefferies' novel to the depopulation of England and the reversion to a wild state. The disaster has destroyed all but the most fragmentary links with the past. Intellectuals and craft workers have abandoned England taking with them knowledge and expertise in science, technology and industry. "Progress", in the sense that Morris uses the word, has gone into reverse. Humanity could therefore be said to be as "in the days of Noë", with the world to begin again. At the time of Jefferies' narrative, however, that rebuilding is only at an early stage and people are living in conditions that are largely early medieval, with some elements of a later feudal organisation. But there is in *After London* none of the idealisation of the Middle Ages to be found in other nineteenth-century texts, no colour or gaiety, no spirit of cooperativeness or Ruskinian pride in work. Only behind strongly defended walls can well-tended private gardens be found; only away from the guile of courts and politics is there refuge from the warfare of a series of city-states. Indeed, most of the groups now inhabiting England are, in Norman Kelvin's apt phrase, "savage, cruel, inhumane and untrustworthy".[23]

The novel's central character is Felix Aquila, who is reminiscent of a romance hero, and has a core belief in the reliability of nature. This belief, as Felix's surname suggests, is strongly attached to the huge sweet-water lake that now occupies the centre of England, and it is across this lake that Felix, frustrated in love and embittered by the failure of society to value his skills as designer and craftsman, sets out in search of a new life. The lake is not altogether pure, however. On its eastern side there lies "a vast stagnant swamp", which is covered by a noxious cloud, emanating from "a thousand years of rottenness" (36, 37).[24] This nightmare of pollution lies over what was once London, and its toxicity increases towards its centre, beneath which lies the heart of the old city. The site is rumoured to contain treasure, but to try to retrieve it means almost certain death, if not by poison gas then at the hands of the demons that are believed to haunt the place. Felix, who sets out in a westerly direction, is blown off course on to the shores of this dead land and abandons his boat to go in search of water.

> He went on, looking for a spring, sometimes walking on firm ground, sometimes sinking to the ankle in a friable soil like black sand. The ground looked, indeed, as if it had been burnt, but there were no charred stumps of timber such as he had seen on the sites of forest fires... In the level plain the desolation was yet more marked; there was not a grass blade or plant; the surface was hard, black, and burned, resembling iron, and indeed in places it resounded to his feet, though he supposed that was the echo from hollow passages below. (202)

The following description of Felix's journey is one of the most extraordinary passages in Victorian fiction. From the past it gathers up elements from saga quests and medieval romances, and from texts as diverse as the *Odyssey* and *The Pilgrim's Progress*. At the same time it anticipates the writing of the early years of the twentieth century, particularly Conrad's tales of colonial predation, accounts of First World War battlefields and passages in Eliot's *The Waste Land*. It describes a psychological as well as a physical location, an internal as well as an external landscape, a testing-ground that requires all Felix's courage, resolve and ingenuity to survive. Partly drugged by poisonous gases, Felix stumbles through this no-man's-land, leaving glowing phosphoric footprints. Skeletons are "drawn upon the black ground in white lines ... as if with a broad piece of chalk", and he is accompanied by clouds "not condensed enough to be visible to direct vision" (203). These forms "shapeless and threatening... like the vague monster of a dream" (204) resemble the soldiers staggering out of gas attacks in Wilfred Owen's poems, or the presence that prompts Eliot's question, "Who is the third who always walks beside you?"[25]

Felix comes to the centre of the land, the heart of the old city, where some walls still stand, but collapse at the touch, allowing glimpses into the abysses of old houses that lie beneath. And when he stumbles across a pile of coins, blackened and filthy like William's in *News from Nowhere,* he realises that the "deserted and utterly extinct city was under his feet" and that "the earth on which he walked... was composed of the mouldered bodies of millions of men who had passed away in the centuries during which the city existed." (206) Felix's exact location in London is of no significance. It derives from Jefferies' inwardness with Felix's experiences, the combination of vividly realised scenes and the representation of Felix's disordered mental state and his struggle for survival.

> He had penetrated into the midst of that dreadful place, of which he heard many a tradition: how the earth was poison, the water poison, the air poison, the very light of heaven, falling through such an atmosphere, poison. There were said to be places where the earth was on fire and belched forth poisonous fumes, supposed to be from the combustion of the enormous stores of strange and unknown chemicals collected by the wonderful people of those times. Upon the surface of the water there was a greenish-yellow oil, to touch which was death to any creature; it was the very essence of corruption. (206)

Jefferies' words seem prophetic, but "the wonderful people of those times" are a deeply ironic reference to his contemporaries. Just as Morris's news from nowhere is delivered to the "somewhere" of 1890, so Jefferies' novel speaks to those who inhabit England before the reversion to wildness prefigured in his novel.

IV

"I'm doing the dearest little serial for Pearson's new magazine, in which I completely wreck and destroy Woking, killing my neighbours in painful and eccentric ways, then proceed via Kingston and Richmond to London, which I sack, selecting South Kensington for feats of particular atrocity."[26] H.G. Wells's letter to Elizabeth Healey was written in 1896 and the "dearest little serial" he was writing was *The War of the Worlds,* one of the many fictions, set in both the immediate and the distant future, in which he destroys London. Wells was born in Kent, lived in Surrey and was educated in the Science Schools at South Kensington, so the relish with which he describes the devastation he plans to wreak on these places perhaps represents an act of imaginative revenge, particularly against dull and timid suburban living. In his scientific romances, however, Wells seems generally to have regarded the area from the Channel Ports up to and including London, as a vast stage on which he could dramatise the destructive effects of time, alien beings, ecological disaster and human folly.

In *The Time Machine,* published in 1895, readers are so engaged with the machine's movements through the fourth dimension, that its location in space tends to be forgotten. Yet its geographical placing is clearly but unemphatically signalled in the text: the Time Traveller lives in Richmond, and there are frequent references to the Thames Valley and allusions to Wimbledon, Wandsworth and Battersea. The Traveller goes so far into the future that there is no possibility of evoking recognisable but altered landmarks and generally Wells is much more concerned with anthropological, political and evolutionary speculation than he is with architecture. Nonetheless, as he hurtles through time, the Traveller glimpses "great and splendid architecture rising about me, more massive than any buildings of our own time, and yet, as it seemed, built of glimmer and mist"; and when he comes to rest by a mysterious, sphinx-like figure he is aware of "other vast shapes — huge buildings with intricate parapets and tall columns" (22–23)[27]. Surveying the Thames Valley from a hilltop, the Time Traveller sees "great palaces dotted about among the variegated greenery, some in ruins and some still occupied" (31). London has disappeared while humanity has differentiated and the Elois have lost energy and purpose.

As he races further into the future, fleeing the Morlocks, the Time Traveller witnesses even greater changes. He finds himself in "a steady twilight" where the air is thin, the sea moves turbidly, the light is dull and he is threatened by huge slow-moving crabs: it is a scene of "abominable desolation" (74, 76). Yet worse is to come when he reaches his final resting place, more than thirty million years in the future:

> ...From the edge of the sea came a ripple and whisper. Beyond these lifeless sounds the world was silent. Silent? It would be hard to convey the stillness of it. All the sounds of man, the bleating of sheep, the cries of birds, the hum of insects, the stir that makes the background of our lives — all that was over...

The Time Traveller witnesses an eclipse and as light begins to return to the world, he is afforded a final vision of the future:

> ...As I stood sick and confused I saw again the moving thing upon the shoal — there was no mistake now that it was a moving thing against the red water of the sea. It was a round thing, the size of a football perhaps, or, it may be, bigger, and tentacles trailed down from it; it seemed black against the weltering blood-red water, and it was hopping fitfully about (77–78).

And the Time Traveller, of course, is still in what was Richmond, surveying the Thames Valley; and that red sea on whose shores there lives only a fitfully hopping sphere, covers the area that was once London.

Fin de siècle, fin du globe. The Time Machine, with its twilit settings, and its aesthetic relish for the shapes, colours and textures of decadence and decay, is characteristic of its period. By 1896, as we have seen, Wells was working on *The War of the Worlds,* published in book form in 1898. Here the Martians sweep up through Surrey, destroy Richmond and converge on London. Wells uses familiar streets and localities of the capital to increase the tension and menace of his narrative. Fugitives from Surrey, bringing with them tales of battles in Chertsey and Weybridge, cross Westminster Bridge, move on to Trafalgar Square, and thence along the Strand. Place names are used with similar effect as a great panic begins:

> ...in the Park terraces and in the hundred other streets of that part of Marylebone, and the Westbourne Park district and St Pancras, and westward and northward in Kilburn and St John's Wood and Hampstead, and eastward in Shoreditch and Highbury and Haggerston and Hoxton, and indeed, through all the vastness of London from Ealing to East Ham (75).

There are glimpses of people being "trampled and crushed... in Bishopsgate Street" (84); Haverstock Hill is blocked by a fallen horse; and Chalk Farm Road choked with refugees. Wells's imaginative engagement with such scenes is signalled by their syntax and the rhythm of clauses and periods. They are deliberately inclusive visions, both topographically and socially comprehensive, so that no metropolitan readers can assume that they will be exempt from disaster.

Towards the end of the novel Wells devotes a chapter to an evocation of "Dead London". The city is covered with black powder and choked by red weeds, full of decaying bodies and skeletons. It has not only become a vast necropolis; it is itself a ghost-like entity, reminiscent of Jefferies' vision:

> London about me gazed at me spectrally. The windows in the white houses were like the eye-sockets of skulls. About me my imagination found a thousand noiseless enemies moving (160).

The narrator does not yet realise that the Martians are already defeated, destroyed by the simple bacteria against which they have no immunity. He climbs to the summit of Primrose Hill and surveys London:

> All about..., and saved as if by a miracle from everlasting destruction, stretched the great Mother of Cities... And as I looked at this wide expanse of houses and factories and churches, silent and abandoned; as I thought of the multitudinous hopes and efforts, the innumerable hosts of lives that had gone to build this human reef, and of the swift and ruthless destruction that had hung over it all; when I realised that the shadow had been rolled back, and that men might still live in the streets, and this dear vast dead city of mine be once more alive and powerful, I felt a wave of emotion that was near akin to tears (162–163).

Such a passage appears to promise renewal, but the novel's final note is not one of reconstruction and celebration. Humanity has learned a lesson: that "we cannot regard this planet as being fenced in and a secure abiding-place for Man; we can never anticipate the unseen good or evil that may come upon us suddenly out of space." (170) Any hope for the future is necessarily temporary and tentative, and for the narrator, even the "busy multitudes" of a repopulated London seem "but the ghosts of the past, haunting the streets that I have seen silent and wretched, going to and fro, phantasms in a dead city, the mockery of life in a galvanised body." (172) This disturbing insight is anticipatory of T.S. Eliot's *The Waste Land* (1922), with its vision of a London crowd: "Unreal City/Under the brown fog of a winter dawn/A crowd flowed over London Bridge, so many/I had not thought death had undone so many."[29]

A similar sense of vulnerability can be found in Wells's *The War in the Air* (1908). Bert Smallways, the novel's protagonist, reflecting on the destruction of New York by airships, realises that "the little island in the silver sea was at the end of its immunity" (203).[30] The subdued echo of John of Gaunt's famous speech in Shakespeare's *Richard II* — "This precious stone set in the silver sea" — emphasises the sense that a long tradition has been brought to an end.[31] The narrator looks back at the events of the book from the safety of "our present world state, orderly, scientific, and secure" but is less concerned with describing that state than with the intervening period, years during which social order collapses and the world re-experiences "Dürer-esque medievalism" (350). Famine and the Purple Death follow, reducing London to a ghost city; and the novel ends with Bert taking his grandson to Crystal Palace from which they look out over a ruined London, whose inhabitants are living at subsistence level. The Crystal Palace, symbolic of Victorian self-belief and faith in progress, now has "splintered pinnacles" and "shattered glass", and gazing at it Bert has "[a] dim, large sense of waste and irrevocable lost opportunities" (359, 377). Although the novel is narrated from the future security of a new world order, it is Bert's experience of suffering and devastation and his sense of loss that makes the strongest impact.

Wells, of course, is often perceived as dealing in gleaming bright futures, and in a range of predictive texts, such as *Anticipations* (1902) or *A Modern Utopia* (1905), he offers versions of a rationally organised future shaped by social and scientific advances. In *When the Sleeper Wakes* (1899), the sleeper's first vision of what appears to be such a future is of "overwhelming architecture" with "[g]igantic globes of cool white light... gossamer suspension bridge[s]... and great archings, circular perforations, balconies... myriads of vast windows." (35)[32] Yet the vision is not benign: small towns and villages have disappeared; electronic communication has replaced most human contact; and old London lies buried beneath the new architecture. The city is now a prison, autocratically ruled, in which the individual life counts for little. Graham, the Sleeper, realises that it is an inevitable development from the Victorian city, whose growth was determined by "the economy of co-operation"; as a result "London is no longer an aggregation of houses but a prodigious hotel" (174).

V

There are some London dreamers who have no need to project themselves into the future. They can conjure a vision of London transfigured, an image of another city that lies behind or beneath the present reality. The only barrier to perceiving this city lies in the limitations of the imagination. William Blake is the supreme London visionary dreamer. At street level he is the engaged observer of inequality and injustice:

> I wander through each chartered street
> Near where the chartered Thames does flow,
> And mark in every face I meet
> Marks of weakness, marks of woe.[33]

Those streets can also become part of a new-built holy city, presiding over a vision of a redeemed world:

> The fields from Islington to Marybone,
> To Primrose Hill and Saint John's Wood,
> Were builded over with pillars of gold;
> And there Jerusalem's pillars stood.[34]

Furthermore, Blake can imagine this miraculous city made great and then polluted and reduced to poverty

> from Lambeth
> We began our foundations, lovely Lambeth! O lovely Hills
> Of Camberwell, we shall behold you no more in glory & pride,
> For Jerusalem lies in ruins and the Furnaces of Los are
> builded there...
> I see London, blind & age bent, begging thro' the Streets
> Of Babylon, led by a child...[35]

Closer to Morris's own time, writers found in London's fogs a medium through which the city may be perceived anew. The celebrated opening of Dickens's *Bleak House* (1852–53) is a good example, with its description of a city physically and metaphorically fog-bound, in which "it would not be wonderful to meet a Megalosaurus, forty feet long or so, waddling like an elephantine lizard up

Holborn-hill."[36] Elizabeth Barrett Browning *in Aurora Leigh* (1856) offers another example, in which the descent of fog appears to expunge the city, or give the effect of a disturbance in the natural course of time:

> ... I saw
> Fog only, the great tawny sweltering fog,
> Involve the passive city, strangle it
> Alive, and draw it off into the void,
> Spires, bridges, streets, and squares, as if a sponge
> Had wiped out London...

Such effects, Browning suggests, are visible to "your city poets", who may thus be "surprised/By a sudden sense of vision and of time."[37]

Auberon Quin, the poet-king of G.K. Chesterton's *The Napoleon of Notting Hill* (1904) is certainly afforded such visions. Although the novel is set in 1984, Chesterton is quick to point out that "London is almost exactly like what it is now" and that the "somewhat depressed reliance upon things happening as they have always happened, which is with all Londoners a mood, has become an assumed condition." (11, 12)[38] Quin recreates the London boroughs as medieval city-states, each governed by a Provost, with guards in splendid liveries. Adam Wayne, the young Provost of Notting Hill, is also a poet who enthusiastically embraces Quin's ideas, and when a new road is proposed that will require the demolition of a street in his borough, he takes military action to protect it. This seems to both Quin and the narrator perfectly natural; as the narrator remarks, "A street is more poetical than a meadow, because a street has a secret. A street is going somewhere and a meadow nowhere." (66) In his poetry, Adam Wayne transforms "the leaden London landscape to a romantic gold", while in his actions "the soul of Notting Hill [has] gone forth and made men realise what it is to live in a city" (71, 149). Such actions validate Quin's outlook, his vision of the reality behind the reality that permeates the novel:

> The light there is on such a day seems not so much to come from the clear heavens as to be a phosphorescence clinging to the shapes themselves. The load of heaven and the clouds is like a load of waters, and the men move like fishes, feeling that they are on the flow of a sea. Everything in a London street completes the fantasy; the carriages and cabs themselves resemble deep-sea creatures with eyes of flame. (13–14)

What is important in such a vision is vision itself, the nature of the act of perception, and in particular the author's mode of regard, his or her ability to shed preconceptions and conventional ideas of what constitutes reality. This idea is well expressed by Arthur Machen when he writes in *The London Adventure* (1924) of "the sense of the eternal mysteries, the eternal beauty hidden beneath the crust of common and commonplace things; hidden and yet burning and glowing continually if you care to look with purged eyes."[39]

VI

Graham in Wells's *When the Sleeper Wakes* falls asleep in the 1890s and awakes in 2100. Contemplating this world of the distant future, he thinks "of the hopes of his vanished contemporaries, and for a moment the dream of London in Morris's quaint old *News from Nowhere*... appeared before him in an atmosphere of infinite loss."[40] It is to that "quaint old" book that I now turn.

In discussions *of News from Nowhere,* emphasis is frequently placed on the second part of the narrative, consisting of William Guest's journey to the Upper Thames, and to the vision of a redeemed Kelmscott Manor as a site of fellowship and repose. Equally significant is the journey that William makes in the first part of the book, eastwards from Hammersmith, through Kensington to Westminster, by way of Piccadilly to Trafalgar Square, Holborn and finally to Bloomsbury and the British Museum. It is from what he observes on this journey, with Dick Hammond's accompanying commentary, that Guest obtains his primary impressions and his first understanding of the priorities and values of the new society. This impression is predominantly topographical and architectural, and lays emphasis on the fate of areas, streets and buildings familiar to Morris's readers. As in the work of H.G. Wells, Morris's use of real names is important — King Street, Hammersmith Broadway, Piccadilly, Endell Street and Oxford Road in this context carry a particular charge, and encourage readers to envisage places they already know transformed by trees, gardens, beautiful buildings and attractive people. Morris is not seeking a sensationalised, shock response — such demolition or relocation as has taken place, Dick's commentary assures us, has arisen from rational, collective decisions deriving from a communal desire for a cleaner and saner life. Morris does not, as Wells so often does, invoke places in order to destroy them at the hands of hostile aliens. There are sharp satirical points, such as the use of part of the Palace of Westminster as a manure store, but the more crucial significance of the transformations that William observes has to do with beauty, grace and elegance. It has also to do with generosity: the people of the future are prepared to retain some buildings that they regard as ugly or inappropriate — like St Paul's Cathedral — whose ruin had been used since the eighteenth century to symbolise the potential decay of London and of English civilisation and influence — they are prepared to preserve secure in the knowledge that they can build better.

William Guest's London journey takes him through the city's former zones of power and elegant society, culminating at the great repository of learning and collective memory, the British Museum. It is here that Old Hammond is able to make a coherent narrative of a history of which Guest and the reader have previously only understood fragments. The journey, however, does not take him any further east than Bloomsbury, so that for the fate of the City and the East End, he has to rely on Hammond's account of "The Clearing of Misery" in the still densely populated area as far as Aldgate, which then thins out into a reclaimed Lea Valley. Such a clearance — effectively a deurbanisation — would have transformed the journey made into central London.

Some reference to an improved East End is vital to Morris's purpose, I think. This area was in the 1880s and 1890s a great testing-ground for social conscience and social action. In Morris's time, the literary tropes most frequently employed in accounts of the East End refer to darkness or descent: the abyss, the whirlpool, the nether world, a pit of disease, filth, horror and danger, from which the inhabitants find it almost impossible to escape.[41] For this benighted place, situated at the centre of darkest England, the location of Jack the Ripper's murders when *News from Nowhere* was written and published; for this city of dreadful night some redemption needed to be imagined, and Morris conceives that redemption in terms of the shared desire for improvement and the relief of misery. Even the comparatively dense population of the City of London, as described by Hammond, represents a kind of reclamation, for areas previously dominated by offices and businesses have been humanised by residence. Furthermore, this detail, conveniently overlooked by most hostile critics of Morris's vision, suggests that he did not shirk the fact that even with a vastly reduced population the mass of London's inhabitants would need to live *somewhere*.

What is perhaps surprising, however, is that by not taking William Guest further east than Bloomsbury, Morris denies himself the opportunity of revisiting in imagination the landscape of his youth. After all, he tells Clara that the time when he best remembers living in the present was "when I was a happy child on a sunny holiday, and had everything that I could think of," (141)[42] and one of his ways of describing the new society is that the world has entered its second childhood. Perhaps for Morris, at that time, the return to Kelmscott Manor was of greatest emotional significance. He creates a version of the Manor uncompromised by Morris's knowledge of Jane's relationship with Rossetti, and reclaims it as a house where, childlike and hand-in-hand with Ellen, he can both recreate the passion of his youth for the natural world and redeem the unhappiness of his middle years. Here, necessity and desire can meet and mingle, and Guest may find the peace and rest he yearns for.

VII

As a coda to this essay, I wish to reflect on some London texts published in and after the year 1910. In the years preceding the First World War, there was a great explosion of "invasion literature", works that, in one form or another, predicted what was now regarded as the almost inevitable coming war with Germany. The volume of such works had been increasing since the 1870s, although at the beginning of this period the likeliest enemy was considered to be France. The titles of many of these works suggest a particular fear for the security of London, as the centre of government and the capital of a widespread political, naval and trading empire. A list of selected titles from 1872 to 1914 tells its own story: *The Commune in London*, *The Siege of London*, *How John Bull Lost London*, *The Monster Municipality*, *The Last Man in London*, *The Capture of London*, *The Doom of the County Council of London*, *London's Peril*, *How the Germans Took London*, *The Storm of London* and *The Ransom for London*. In his bibliography of future fictions Ian Clarke describes many more which, without having London in their title, are specifically concerned with a threat to the capital.[43]

Elsewhere, observers were considering the capital's internal problems, deriving from its massive and rapid expansion. The years around 1910 saw an intensification of interest in "the Condition-of-England Question", a term revived from the 1840s, and the title of a book by C.F.G. Masterman, published in 1909.[44] Masterman was a Liberal MP who eventually served in the Cabinet and who had been concerned about the conditions suffered by the great mass of London's population. After living for a while in Camberwell he published, in 1902, *From the Abyss: Of its Inhabitants by One of Them.* He was also concerned, as this extract from an essay published in 1901 demonstrates, what living in such circumstances might mean for the future:

> ...the inevitable isolation and loneliness of the competing units in a monstrous aggregation such as London, and the absence of a background setting present action, however obscure, into some large framework of meaning, and enforcing on the individual the sense of immediate personal responsibility — these are the general conditions which are filling observers of the ghetto with dreary forebodings for the future.[45]

And in *The Condition of England* Masterman takes up the idea of the inevitable decline of great cities, along with the empires over which they rule:

> And as of Nineveh there remains but a heap, and of Tyrus a spit of sandy shore... so a triumphant imagination can fling off the yoke of the present, to see in solid England dynamic instead of static forces, and all the cities in motion and flow towards some unknown ends... Nor does any consolation reside in the fact that one day, great London itself will become but a vast tomb for all its busy people, and of its splendour and pride not one stone be left upon another...[46]

Masterman was a friend and associate of E.M. Forster, who saw his *Howards End* (1910) as a contribution to the "Condition-of-England" debate. London is seen in the novel as the obverse of Howards End, the house that represents rootedness, continuity and an organic relationship with the natural world. For the culturally-minded Schlegels, the city may afford opportunities for music, art and "civilised" discussion; but, it is no fit place for living a balanced, humane life. Leonard Bast, the doomed insurance clerk, has migrated to the city and lives in a block of flats "constructed with extreme cheapness", part of the landscape of "bricks and mortar rising and falling with the restlessness of the water in a fountain, as the city receives more and more men upon her soil." (59)[47] He is one of the army of clerks serving London's expanding financial sector, living in the new suburbs south of the river. Trapped in a loveless relationship, he is marooned in the city, cut off from his rural beginnings and unable to realise his educational ambitions.

London in *Howards End* represents a peculiarly modern style of civilisation. Margaret Schlegel, the true heir of Howards End, notes in its streets "the architecture of hurry" and hears "the language of hurry on the mouths of its inhabitants" (116). The possession of land has given way to the ownership of movable goods and modern society is once again a "nomadic horde", a "civilisation of luggage", and future historians, Forster comments, will note how "the middle class accreted possessions without taking root in the earth, and may find in this the secret of their imaginative poverty" (154). By the end, with most of the surviving characters grouped at Howards End, London appears as "a red rust" — a line advancing across the meadows, threatening the rootedness of life in the house. "London's creeping," remarks Helen Schlegel, "and London is only part of something else... Life's going to be melted down, all over the world." (329) London's inexorable approach, almost certainly in the form of those cockneyfied villas that Morris so much deplored, seems to be the vanguard of a loss in the quality of life, of the seeking out and destruction of quiet places, of the reduction to a simple, undifferentiated homogeneity of all that is individual and complex. Margaret's reply "This craze for motion has only set in during the last hundred years. It may be followed by a civilisation that won't be a movement, because it will rest on the earth" is desperately optimistic but barely consolatory (329).

In Virginia Woolf's *Mrs Dalloway* (1925) a recurring motif is a closed car that may or may not contain the Prime Minister, or even the Queen, a circumstance that leads to a narrative reflection on the future of London:

> ... there could be no doubt that greatness was seated within; greatness was passing, hidden, down Bond Street, removed only by a hand's-breadth from ordinary people who might now, for the first and last time, be within speaking distance of the majesty of England, of the enduring symbol of the state which will be known to curious antiquaries, sifting the ruins of time, when London is a grass-grown path and all those hurrying along the pavement this Wednesday morning are but bones with a few wedding rings mixed up in their dust and the gold stoppings of innumerable decayed teeth. The face in the motor-car will then be known.[48]

This vision of future decay occurs in a novel that is notable for Clarissa Dalloway's celebration of London, her pleasure in familiar streets, her sense of being at home in the city. In a more combative spirit, D.H. Lawrence argued with Bertrand Russell about the difference between facts and truths: London, he maintained, was a fact but not a truth and if people only realised this they would destroy the city. For Lawrence, London became a City of Dissolution, a location of unreality and ghost-like presences, as he wrote in his poem, "People":

> The ripeness of these apples of night
> Distilling over me
> Makes sickening the white
> Ghost-flux effaces that hie
> Them endlessly, endlessly by
> Without meaning or reason why
> They ever should be.[49]

This sense of an Unreal City anticipates T.S. Eliot's in one of the central texts of literary modernism, The *Waste Land* (1922), in lines I have already quoted:

> Unreal City,
> Under the brown fog of a winter dawn,
> A crowd flowed over London
> Bridge, so many,
> I had not thought death had undone so many.[50]

And Russell himself entertained similar visions:

> I used to have strange visions of London as a place of unreality. I used in imagination to see bridges collapse and sink, and the whole great city vanish like a morning mist. Its inhabitants began to seem like hallucinations, and I would wonder whether the world I thought I had loved was a mere product of my own febrile nightmares.[51]

In Forster, a wish to hold London at bay; in Woolf, a momentary anticipation of a time when the city will have returned to nature; in Lawrence and Eliot a sense of a place inhabited by ghostly presences; in Russell a city that seems to dissolve before his eyes. It seems so easy to dream a transfigured London or, voluntarily or involuntarily, to watch it disappear.

VIII

How does one distinguish Morris's vision of a future London from the others discussed in this essay? For me, the crucial point is that the city experienced by William Guest has taken shape as a result of a desired change, formed by the collective will of men and women thinking and acting in accordance with a desire for peace, harmony and beauty. Although violent unrest is a necessary part of the historical evolution towards this change, the city's transformation has not been effected by disaster or invasion; it has taken place by consent and has been completed cooperatively. It lacks that element of enforcement, that sense of a troubling hallucination or dissolution, or those feelings of fear, danger and vulnerability that mark so many fictions of the future city. This is not to say that Morris conceives of his new society as static or as immune to change for the worse. As that wise woman Ellen points out: "Who knows? happy as we are, times may alter; we may be bitten with some impulse towards change, and many things may seem too wonderful for us to resist, too exciting not to catch at, if we do not know that they are but phases of what has gone before; and withal ruinous, deceitful and sordid."[52] As Ellen also knows, William Guest's sojourn in this new world of peace and rest can only be a brief one, and his fading from the narrative of the future is almost unbearably poignant. Yet, overwhelmingly, it is a text marked by hope. For us, reading *News from Nowhere,* a century after its composition, that hope should be sustaining. A hope that should seem no less potent if we find ourselves sharing some of William's own yearning as he sits deep beneath the city in the underground railway: "If I could but see a day of it ... if I could but see it!"[53]

Richmond-on-Thames, Delhi and Nottingham
November 2003–October 2006

Notes

1. William Morris, "Prologue: the Wanderers", *The Earthly Paradise* (1868–70), ed. J.W. Mackail, 4 vols, (London: Longman, Green & Co, 1905), vol. I, p.3.
2. William Morris, *News from Nowhere* (1890), ed. Krishan Kumar (Cambridge: Cambridge University Press, 1995), p.3.
3. Morris's review of *Looking Backward* was contributed to *Commonweal* June 1889, and reprinted in May Morris, *William Morris: Artist, Writer, Socialist* (Oxford: Basil Blackwell, 1936), II, p.502.
4. Letter to Sir Horace Mann, 24 November 1774, *Horace*

Walpole's Correspondence, ed. W.S. Lewis, 48 vols. vol. 24 (New Haven and London: Yale University Press and Oxford University Press, 1967), p.62.

5. "Common Sense" [Sir Richard Phillips], *Monthly Magazine,* February 1811; quoted in B.I. Coleman (ed), *The Idea of the City in Nineteenth Century Britain* (London: Routledge & Kegan Paul, 1973), p.39.
6. Anna Laetitia Barbauld, *Eighteen Hundred and Eleven, A Poem* (1812), quoted in X. Baron (ed), *London 1066–1914: Literary Sources and Documents,* 3 vols (Robertsbridge, East Sussex: Helm Information, 1997), vol. II, pp.120–122.
7. "Dedication" to *Peter Bell the Third, The Complete Poetical Works of Percy Bysshe Shelley,* ed. Thomas Hutchinson (London: Oxford University Press, 1935), p.343.
8. W.M. Thackeray, *Vanity Fair* (1847–48), ed. John Sutherland (London: Penguin Books, 2001), p.585.
9. T.B. Macaulay, *Review of The Ecclesiastical and Political History of the Popes of Rome, during the Sixteenth and Seventeenth Centuries,* by Leopold Ranke, *Edinburgh Review,* CXLV (October 1840), p.228.
10. G.A. Sala, *Twice Round the Clock* (1858); quoted in Baron, II, p.335.
11. Mary Elizabeth Braddon, *Aurora Floyd* (1862–63), ed. P.D. Edwards (Oxford: Oxford University Press, 1996), p.27.
12. Nathaniel Hawthorne, *Our Old Home* (1863); quoted in Baron, II, p.799.
13. Letter to Mark Lemon, 2 July 1856, *The Letters of Charles Dickens,* 12 vols. vol. 8, ed. Graham Storey and Kathleen Tillotson (Oxford: Clarendon Press, 1995), p.143.
14. His illustrations for Dante's *Inferno* were published in 1861, those for the *Bible* in 1866, and for Tennyson's *Idylls of the Kingin* 1868–69. Since 1867 his work had been on show in his own gallery in Bond Street.
15. Gustave Doré and Blanchard Jerrold, *London: a Pilgrimage* (1872; New York: Dover Publications, 1970), p.172.
16. The lines are from Poe's lyric, "To Helen", first published in 1831.
17. Trollope began writing the book after the critical success of *The Warden* (1855) was not immediately matched by its popularity with the public, and he was discouraged from continuing with its successor, *Barchester Towers* (1857). Longman rejected the manuscript and although Trollope continued to revise the text in 1855–56, his career as a novelist had now begun to gather momentum and the psychological moment had passed for a work commenting on

the strengths and weaknesses of mid-century English society. The 1972 text was edited by N.J. Hall and published by Oxford University Press; it was reissued by the Trollope Society in 1995. For information on how Trollope may have used parts of his manuscript in other works see Hall's Introduction pp. XX—XXI. The remainder of the Introduction is largely devoted to showing how Trollope's concerns as expressed in *The New Zealander* are manifested in his fiction up until his death in 1882. Page references in the next three paragraphs are to the Trollope Society edition.

18. Although it is known that Trollope wrote a chapter on the Civil Service, it is absent from the extant manuscript; see Hall's Introduction p. XX for an explanation of this lacuna.
19. Richard Jefferies, "The Modern Thames", *The Open Air* (London: J.M. Dent, 1914), p.113.
20. Letter to Georgiana Burne-Jones, 28 April 1855, *The Collected Letters of William Morris,* ed. Norman Kelvin, 4 vols (Princeton, NJ: Princeton University Press, 1985–1996), vol. II, p.426.
21. *Ibid*, p.427, n.i.
22. *Ibid*, p.436.
23. *Ibid*, p.427, n.i.
24. Richard *Jefferies, After London; or, Wild England* (1885; Oxford: Oxford University Press, 1980). All page references in the next three paragraphs are to this edition.
25. TS. Eliot, "What the Thunder Said", *The Waste Land,* 1. 359, *Collected Poems 1909–1962* (London: Faber & Faber, 1966), p.77.
26. H.G. Wells to Elizabeth Healey [late Spring 1896], *The Correspondence of H.G. Wells,* Volume I, 1880–1903, ed. David C. Smith (London: Pickering & Chatto, 1998), p.261.
27. H.G. Wells, "The Time Machine" (1895), *Selected Short Stories* (Harmondsworth: Penguin Books, 1958). All page references in the next two paragraphs are to this edition.
28. H.G. Wells, *The War of the Worlds* (1898; London: J.M. Dent, 1993). All page references in the next two paragraphs are to this edition.
29. "The Burial of the Dead", *The Waste Land,* II. 60–63, *Collected Poems,* p.65.
30. H.G. Wells, *The War in the Air* (1908: London: T. Nelson & Co, n.d). All page references in this paragraph are to this edition.
31. William Shakespeare, *King Richard* II(1595), 2.1.46, ed. Charles R. Forker (London: Arden Shakespeare, 2002), p.246.

32. H.G. Wells, *When the Sleeper Wakes* (1899) ed. John Lawton (London: J.M. Dent, 1994). All page references in this paragraph are to this edition.
33. William Blake, "London", *Songs of Innocence and of Experience* (1794), *The Poems of William Blake,* ed. W.H. Stevenson (London: Longman, 1971), p.213.
34. *Jerusalem,* Fourth Chapter, Plate 84, II. 3-6,11-12, op. cit, p.678.
35. *Jerusalem,* Second Chapter, Plate 27, II. 19-22, op. cit, p.678.
36. Charles Dickens, *Bleak House* (1852–53), ed. Stephen Gill (Oxford: Oxford University Press, 1996), p. II.
37. Elizabeth Barrett Browning, *Aurora Leigh* (1856), Book in, II. 178–76,199–200, ed. Kerry McSweeney (Oxford: Oxford University Press, 1993), p.80.
38. G.K. Chesterton, *The Napoleon of Notting Hill* (1904), ed. Bernard Bergonzi (Oxford: Oxford University Press, 1994). All page references in this paragraph are to this edition.
39. Arthur Machen, *The London Adventure* (New York: Alfred A. Knopf, 1924), pp. 91–92.
40. *When the Sleeper Wakes,* p.120.
41. Contemporary titles include William Booth, *In Darkest England* (1890), Jack London, *The People of the Abyss* (1903), George Gissing, *The Nether World* (1889), Arthur Morrison, *Tales of Mean Streets* (1894) and Henry W. Nevinson, *Neighbours of Ours* (1895). Peter Keating's anthology *Working Class Stories of the 1890s* (London: Routledge & Kegan Paul, 1971) offers a good introduction to the London fiction of that decade.
42. Morris, *News from Nowhere,* p.141.
43. See Ian Clarke, *The Tale of the Future from the Beginning to the Present Day: an Annotated Bibliography,* 2nd edition (London: The Library Association, 1972). Other titles by Professor Clarke on this subject are: *Voices Prophesying War 1763–1984* (Oxford: Oxford University Press, 1964) and *The Patterns of Expectation, 1644–2001* (London: Jonathan Cape, 1979). He has also edited two anthologies of turn-of-the-century invasion literature: *The Tale of the Next Great War, 1871–1914* (Liverpool: Liverpool University Press, 1995) and *The Great War with Germany, 1800–1014* (Liverpool: Liverpool University Press, 1997).
44. The phrase is, of course, Thomas Carlyle's: it is the title of the first chapter *of Chartism* (1839) and is discussed again in *Past and Present* (1843). Carlyle's plea for a more sympathetic insight into the lives and aspirations of the mass of the population was most fully met by the "industrial", "factory"

or "social problem" novels of such writers as Charles Dickens, Benjamin Disraeli, Elizabeth Gaskell, Charles Reade and Charlotte Elizabeth Tonna.

45. C.F.G. Masterman, "Realities at Home", *The Heart of the Empire: Discussions of Problems of Modern City Life in England* (1901); quoted in Coleman pp. 208–09.
46. C.F.G. Masterman, *The Condition of "England"* (1909), ed. J.T. Boulton (London: Methuen, 1960), p.222.
47. E.M. Forster, *Howards End (1910),* ed. Oliver Stallybrass (Harmondsworth: Penguin Books, 1975), p.59. All page references in this and the following paragraph are to this edition.
48. Virginia Woolf, *Mrs Dalloway* (1925), ed. Stella McNichol (London: Penguin Books, 1992), pp. 17–18.
49. *The Complete Poems of D.H. Lawrence,* ed. Vivian de Sola Pinto and Warren Roberts (1964; London: Heinemann, 1972), p.252. Lawrence made this poem and "Street Lamps", also concerned with the dissolution of the city, in 1917, deriving them from a single poem "The Street Lamps", first written in 1910 or 1911.
50. Eliot, op. cit., *ibid.*
51. Bertrand Russell, *Autobiography* (1967–69). One-volume edition, (London: George Allen and Unwin.1978), p.241.
52. Morris, *News from Nowhere,* p.202.
53. *Ibid*, p.4.

A Tramp's Utopia
The Big Rock Candy Mountains
*Haywire Mac**

One evenin' as the sun went down
And the jungle fire was burnin'
Down the track came a hobo hikin',
And he said: Boys I'm not turnin',
I'm headed fer a land that's far away
Beside the crystal fountains,
So come with me, we'll all go see
The Big Rock Candy Mountains.

In the Big Rock Candy Mountains,
There's a land that's fair and bright,
Where the handouts grow on bushes,
And you sleep out every night.
Where the boxcars are all empty,
And the sun shines every day
On the birds and the bees and the cigarette trees,
And the lemonade springs where the bluebird sings,
In the Big Rock Candy Mountains.

In the Big Rock Candy Mountains,
All the cops have wooden legs,
The bulldogs all have rubber teeth,
And the hens lay soft-boiled eggs.
The farmers' trees are full of fruit,
And the barns are full of hay.
Oh, I'm bound to go where there ain't no snow,
Where the rain don't pour, the wind don't blow,
In the Big Rock Candy Mountains.

---

*There are various version of this song. This version was taken from Marie Louise Berneri's *Journey Through Utopia*

In the Big Rock Candy Mountains,
You never change your socks,
And the little streams of alcohol
Come tricklin' down the rocks.
There the brakemen have to tip their hats
And the railroad bulls are blind.
There's a lake of stew and of whisky too,
You can paddle all around 'em in a big canoe,
In the Big Rock Candy Mountains.

In the Big Rock Candy Mountains,
All the jails are made of tin,
And you can bust right out again
As soon as you are in.
There ain't no short-handled shovels,
No axes, saws or picks.
I'm going to stay where you sleep all day,
Where they hung the Turk that invented work,
In the Big Rock Candy Mountains.

Steep Step Stroud and Wondrous Whiteway

Jeff Cloves

I have a much-thumbed Paladin paperback (1978) of Gillian Darley's inspirational *Villages of Vision: a study of strange utopias* and, along with William Morris' *News From Nowhere* and his only play *The Tables Turned or Nupkins Awakened* (a satirical sketch pre-dating *News from Nowhere*), it's my starting point for this bit of subjective local exploration. In his foreword to the Five Leaves' 2007 edition of *Villages of Vision*, David McKie writes: "Sometimes the motives of the creators... as with Robert Owen's mixed bag of creations, or the mostly doomed enterprises of the Chartists, or that source of so much early 20th century outrage, Whiteway in Gloucestershire, the impetus was political-cum-ideological."

It is Whiteway Colony's political-cum-ideological impetus which engages me, as it once engaged my mum and dad at the end of WW2. Dad, a sheet-metal worker, had been directed circa 1940 to work at Gloster Aircraft for the duration and there he joined the Communist Party. Branch meetings were held in our requisitioned flat in Cheltenham under the unlikely chairmanship of one Lord Wogan Phillips. Mum (a dressmaker) and dad were set to return to their semi in East Barnet when the war ended but one Sunday in 1945 they pedalled their tandem up the precipitous Birdlip Hill and set off for Miserden to take a peek at its nearby Whiteway Colony. For one afternoon they gave thought to living there. At that time the Colony (six miles from Stroud) was without mains power and sewage and, what with its somewhat lurid reputation locally, I fancy it was a bit too much for their working class puritanism. Their roots in modest suburbia — plus their instinct to be close to their ageing parents, all still living in E17 — drew mum and dad back to the end of the Piccadilly Line.

So, I didn't spend my formative years among the arty pacifist anarchic vegetarian free-love nude bohemians of Whiteway but instead passed the 11+ to East Barnet Grammar and, five years later, emerged fully prepared for conventional middle-class life. In 1999, however, I moved to Stroud and have been there ever since. It wasn't my plan. I fell in love with Cheltenham as a child and originally intended to live there. Then Stroud took hold. The last time the much-mourned poet, Adrian Mitchell, performed in Stroud he stayed with us and left me this hand-written line: *There's something strange about Stroud.* 'Put it in a poem Jeff,' he said, and maybe I will one day. Maybe I already have.

I'd written a poem (an attempt at self-fulfilling prophecy based largely on hearsay) about the strangeness of Stroud seven years before I moved there. Whiteway's communards, and their infectious radicalism, got a respectful mention. I'm no historian or academic, but repeated trips to Stroud to visit my friend the anarchist/pacifist/poet/publisher/pamphleteer/letterpress printer, Dennis Gould, had alerted me to the reality that, strangely, Stroud was and is a festering radical boil on the Tory bum of Royalist Gloucestershire. There had to be causes for this anomaly, I reasoned, so Stroud triumphed over Cheltenham.

Stroud RiffRaff RipRap

the people's flag is deepest green[1]
small is beautiful they say
the banks are full of bottles
money's had its day[2]
now it's mutual aid exchange and mart
re-cycling — that's the way
poll tax claims turn to compost

so resist and disobey!
the sheep are in the meadow
the cows are in the corn
New-Agers are in therapy
there's yoga on the lawn
Queen May holds court on Pagan Hill
King Harvest reigns in Hyde
there's a ley-line straight to Avalon[3]
by way of Mendip side

rap it!
steep step Stroud[4]
head up in a cloud
feet down in the old canal
wool mill in a shroud

ecologists on Castle Street[5]
earth mothers in the town
vegetarians in The Shambles[6]
Peace Convoy on the down[7]
the piano factory blazes[8]
phoenix Pelican resounds[9]
rockanroll band in its back bar
while poets stand their ground[10]
in Slad in Edge in Piedmont
a production line of verse
while the dole queue gets much longer
and the slump gets worse and worse
hospitals and schools close down
farm land is set aside
for theme park golf course country club
and the hungry are denied

rap it!
steep step Stroud
head up in a cloud
feet down in the old canal[11]
wool mill in a shroud[12]

come Leveller and Digger
eco-freak anarcho-punk
pagan Rudolf Steiner-ite[13]
communard[14] and Prinknash monk[15]
green councillor utopian
feminist stoned dope-head
you dispossessed and riff-raff[16]
with no job no roof no bed
millennium approaches[17]
change is in the air
the seasons have their cycles
hope's the enemy of despair
in Stroud there's something stirring
on the wold the wind is sweet
it's blowing down from Whiteway
and sweeping through the streets
of steep step Stroud
head up in a cloud
feet down in the old canal
wool mill in a shroud

steep step Stroud
rap it long and loud
'til they have built Jerusalem
in steep step Stroud

This key (for non-Stroudies) was published together with the poem on a broadsheet I made and photo-printed in 1992:

[1] Of 24 town councillors 12 are Greens
[2] Visionary cits have launched a no-money economy (LETS)
[3] A mystical-radical grid links centres of cosmic consciousness
[4] Gary Snyder's zen poem *Riprap* notes: 'cobble of the milky way'
[5] Would-be Green MP Sue Atkinson and Green Town Mayor John Marjoram
[6] The Shambles Market in ancient quarter of the town
[7] New Age traveller-refugees from the Bean Field police

attack at Stonehenge in 1988

[8] Burned down 1989 — see Laurie Lee's *Cider with Rosie*

[9] Caught fire 1990 — 'Duckhams', the pub dog, it was that died

[10] Laurie Lee Slad: Dennis Gould Edge: Mike, Frances, and Adam Horovitz: Piedmont

[11] Abandoned Stroudwater Canal disappears into Sapperton Tunnel

[12] Stroud's five valleys once supported some 300 wool mills

[13] Green children go to Wynstones (Steiner) School near Gloucester

[14] Whiteway: Tolstoyan-anarchist community near Miserden

[15] Prinknash Dominican Abbey/poet Dom Sylvester Houédard (d.1992)

[16] Dennis Gould has used the title *RiffRaff* for over twenty years

[17] New Age publishers *Gaia* are based in Stroud

I imagined this rap would sound incredibly dated twenty years on but little has changed politically and it holds. Half the Windsor family still lives locally but now thirteen out of eighteen town councillors are Green and the canal is undergoing (partial) restoration. The LETS scheme petered out and *Stroud Pounds* are yet to establish. *Gaia* moved away and the Newlab MP, who swept in with Blair, was defeated in the 2010 election.

Meanwhile, I've come to know the Whiteway Colony somewhat. My children attended the playgroup held in its community hall, each year we've visited its lovely fête (with free swimming in its communal pool) and I've been to various meetings and poetry and music events there. With its timber structure, shallow-pitched corrugated roof and wooden verandah, the hall looks like a misplaced outpost of the British Raj. The finger-post on the Miserden Road which points to 'The Colony Hall' nails it perfectly. Actually its own story fits Whiteway's radical literary history to a tee — so here it is.

About three miles from the Colony, the Cranham TB Sanatorium was founded by a Dr Pruen in 1899 — a year after the Colony. His instincts, if not utopian, were certainly visionary. He prescribed fresh air, exercise and good food, and the valiant sufferers sometimes slept out on the open verandahs of the wooden chalets. The post-WW2 availability of streptomycin put an end to dependence on fresh air and the sanatorium closed in 1956. Much earlier though, in 1925, the Colonists — themselves puritanical adherents to fresh air, exercise and healthy diet — seized the day, bought a redundant chalet, dismantled it and transported it to Whiteway. There they adapted and rebuilt it as their unique Colony Hall. But there's a further twist to this tale and it involves that curious radical (but no utopian) George Orwell. He was a patient at Cranham from January 1949 to September 1949 and while there he reputedly put the finishing touches to his novel of dystopia, *1984*. He died in hospital in 1950. His life is further linked to Whiteway but firstly, we need to go back nearly seventy years before the Colony was founded.

In 1831, brother and sister Mary and James Greaves, who were high-born converts to so-called Sacred Socialism, decided that the village of Randwick (three miles from Stroud) was in need of their reforming zeal. Determined to relieve the distress of destitute wool trade weavers they instituted their own 'Social Service' scheme. This was influenced somewhat by Robert Owen's New Lanark experiment and the advanced educational theories of Pestalozzi. Thus the Greaveses laboured to impose a form of mutualism whereby the villagers worked communally to set the decaying village to rights. Tokens were given in payment for this work, which were exchangeable for food, clothes, tools, furniture and improving books. It had the ring of a well-meaning experiment in which the poor were still taught to know their place, and foundered after two years. Still, maybe something in the intellectual/radical soil around Stroud attracted the Greaveses, and in 1898 a bunch of Tolstoyan anarchists who'd decamped from Croydon, were similarly attracted.

Christian in belief, the ten (all single) founding pioneers bought forty-two acres of land near Miserden, and lived in tents, or at the local pub and elsewhere, while they built their own rudimentary wooden huts and set about achieving their utopian dreams of common ownership, self-sufficiency, and moral scruple. That Whiteway — the oldest surviving secular community in Britain — still exists with many of its ideals intact is, I suppose, some kind of miracle, and one of its founding principles is even enshrined in law. The colonists insisted — they ceremonially burned the freehold document — that the Colony land be held in common by all who lived there. So, departing colonists could sell only their plot-lander dwellings, but not the land on which they stood. In 1955, when one such tried to sell hers, together with the land beneath and around it, the Colonists rose up in defence of principle and eventually, and paradoxically, the dispute went to court. The colonists won the day.

There are many influences and strands which may or may not have contributed to Stroud's radical cussedness: the influx of notably independent Flemish weavers on which the wool trade depended, Luddite outbreaks of farm machinery breaking as Captain Swing rode by, and inevitably, West Country Methodism. But these factors can be applied to Gloucestershire as a whole, and yet there's no other Stroud in this huge county. Only Stroud has a Whiteway. And Stroud was, and is, not your average chocolate box Cotswold town. Its 19th and 20th century concentration of engineering industry made it, in effect, an outpost of the South Midlands and gave it a different flavour. And then there's the influx of late 19th century Arts and Crafts people heavily influenced by the self-proclaimed communist but distinctly anarchic William Morris. Furniture was hand-made at the Arts and Crafts outpost in Sapperton and the Arts and Crafts Movement clings on stubbornly, not only in Stroud but in Chipping Camden and elsewhere in the county. In 1922 the Cotswold Co-operative Handicrafts Guild was established at Whiteway. There are still Arts and Crafts practitioners resident there now.

Nowadays, Stroud has become a fashionable resort-cum-home for TV thesps and celebs. My sons report sightings of the Sheriff of Nottingham in the High Street and I see loaded sitcom heroines waiting at local supermarket check-outs. The arrival some years ago of Damien Hirst and his army of assistants has provoked an influx of arty technicians from London but Stroud and Whiteway's literary history, goes back, at least, to the twenties.

In Stroud now, many well-known and market-successful writers, poets, painters, potters, constructors and sculptors, photographers and film-makers, comprise an arty community larger, I suspect, than St Ives in its heyday. Collectively, their impetus is not notably political-cum-ideological, unless you regard the teachings of Rudolf Steiner as such. The Steiners are an undeniable presence — though not at Whiteway I suspect — and now own Stroud's original fantastical Ruskin-influenced art school and other once-public buildings. The Christian Steiners are a closed book to me, but Wynstones School, which was founded in 1935 with the support of teachers who'd fled Nazi Germany, certainly draws parents with school-age children to live in Stroud and I find many Steiner attitudes towards education very appealing. The Steiners also do admirable work with troubled and disadvantaged young people and to the bureaucrats at the Department of Education, their impetus may even seem utopian.

Broadly speaking, spirituality is big in Stroud and there is much in its collective psyche which leaves me bemused: tarot, I Ching, homoeopathy, acupuncture, alternative treatments of every known kind, crystals, foot massage, a variety of yogas — the list is endless. It often seems there are more therapists here than people, and many cits appear capable of believing anything. If I invented my own plausibly vague religion, published an exquisitely-designed text and distributed it among Stroud's centres of consciousness, I fancy I'd have a posse of followers in no time. If I was young, good-looking, and artistically gifted, God only knows how big my church might become.

Characteristically, Whiteway has always been home and sanctuary for artists and craftworkers, conscientious objectors, Spanish republican/anarchist refugees from the civil war, free-thinkers and British anarchists of all stripes, and has nurtured the extraordinary literary and political links between Stroud and Andalusia in particular. The pacifist anarchist feminist Lilian Woolf (1875–1974) lived at Whiteway with her companion Tom Keell — editor of the anarchist newspaper *Freedom* — for ten years and founded a wholefood shop there. During the Spanish Civil War *Freedom* became *Spain and the World* and in 1939 changed its name again to *War Commentary*. It reverted to *Freedom* in 1945. Whiteway Colony was variously the publishing address of Freedom Press and storehouse of its literature while Tom Keell lived there. Lilian was the Colony's secretary for many years and later ran a wholefood shop in Stroud. Tom Keell died in 1938 but Lilian stayed on and lived at the Colony for over forty years. In 1945, the then editors of *Freedom* were sent to prison for sedition and inciting returning troops to disaffect. The anarchist poet and educational theorist, Herbert Read (later knighted) and George Orwell were centrally involved in setting up The Freedom Press Defence Committee.

I took a walk around Whiteway recently. There's barely a physical trace left of the do-it-yourself plotlander environment so beloved of the late Colin Ward. Conversely, some of the spreads have a touch of the Ponderosa Ranch about them. So, no beach-hut picturesque then and there's not one dwelling left with the appeal and style of the Colony Hall. The longevity of Whiteway warms me cockles even so and, although I have no more than anecdotal evidence and collective memory to go by, I like to think — and believe — that Whiteway's radicalism has seeped into Stroud's consciousness. Whiteway's longest residing colonist, Joy Evans, who was born there in 1924, is certainly a keeper of the utopian flame but it's unclear — at least to me — whether the Tolstoyan anarchism of its pioneers still informs the life and times of Whiteway now.

I don't detect a generalised over-arching utopianism in Stroud either. Far from it, but there's certainly a strong feeling of community even though there exists a cultural and social apartheid too obvious to ignore. In crude terms, the middle-class green arty crafties of Upper Stroud and the hoi polloi of Lower Stroud might as well live in separate towns. And even among the Upper-Stroudies, I'm startled by the lack of *conscious* awareness of Whiteway and interest in its ideals. Nevertheless, despite the dire years of New Labour's determination to equate 'Public' with second-rate and 'Private' with the Earthly Paradise, its insistence that Newlab wasn't driven by ideology but concerned only with 'what works' (works for whom? we ask), and its denial of the words *socialism, idealism,* and *utopia,* Stroud stubbornly resisted. It mounted a terrific campaign against the Iraq war, has announced itself a 'Transition Town', hosts a vigorous pro-cycling action group and, in 2012, Stroud District Council's proposal to allow 1500 new houses on a green field site, prompted the immediate establishment of the Don't Strangle Stroud campaign. Meanwhile, active support of Public Libraries and the NHS is ongoing.

Stroud has a clear sense of self-identity, is friendly, co-operative, imaginative, adaptable, more tolerant than me, and frequently quite barmy. Despite having a Tory MP, its spirit, I insist, derives above all from the Whiteway Colony.

***

una aventura

Lorca is walking to Whiteway
he is charmed by all he sees
his chanced-upon companion
lives there it turns out
young and sunburned — she is
if you believe local lore
committed to free-love
nudism and vegetarian picnics
is a witch very likely

fortune favours Federico
¡es un milagro!
she speaks Spanish
and looks lovely as a lark
he is ready to fall in love
with Whiteway
with her
with all the young men
he is yet to meet

Stroud's hills are green and lush
not scraped and sparse
olive trees are unknown
she tells him tales
of Tolstoy and peaceful Christianity
they plod like pilgrims
forever uphill
Lorca is on his way
to visit *compadres*
in another county
but he's been waylaid
and led astray
he has wandered
from his path
or has he found it?
what happens at Whiteway
is a closed book

what will happen later
is forever unknown

days later still dreaming
Lorca crosses the Atlantic
aboard a Lorca liner deluxe
the Statue of Liberty beckons
he is in for
one helluva shock*

The writer, traveler, Hispanicist and associate of the Bloomsbury Set, Gerald Brenan (1894-1987), lived briefly at Miserden village before departing to walk to China. He never got there. Instead, he lived most of his life in Spain and wrote *The Spanish Labyrinth, The Face of Spain* and *South from Granada.* He was known at Whiteway and (I suspect) inspired Laurie Lee — who played his fiddle at Whiteway's dances — to set out 'one midsummer morning', to walk to Spain. Laurie Lee fought with the British International Brigade in Spain and his magnificent account of those times, *A Moment of War*, completed his autobiographical trilogy which began with *Cider With Rosie*. He was an admirer of Federico García Lorca and his early poems in particular are held to be much influenced by him.

The Orwell connection to Stroud links him to Laurie Lee, Whiteway and the anarchist paper *Freedom* via Spain. His great book *Homage to Catalonia* is the basis of Ken Loach's film *Land and Freedom,* which gives a sympathetic picture of Spanish anarchists.

For the whole of my life so far, civil war has raged somewhere in the world, and there seems no end in sight. Seventy-five years ago in Spain, the army led by General Franco staged a military coup against the legally elected Republican government and the resulting civil war lasted for nearly three years. Franco's army — boosted by the

---

*Lorca made a brief visit to England on his way to the USA in 1929 and travelled to Hereford. I like to think he went there via Stroud and visited Whiteway.

support of Hitler and Mussolini — eventually triumphed and his dictatorship survived from 1939 until 1975. The political/social/cultural fallout from this bitter conflict continues yet, and the great poet dramatist and musician, Federico García Lorca, remains a central and iconic figure in its story.

Lorca was murdered by a Fascist assassination squad in the first weeks of the Spanish Civil War in August 1936. He was gay, famous, fêted, a staunch republican and, in every way, an affront to the Catholic conservative political right. But he was just one among the countless republicans murdered and imprisoned during and after Franco's military coup and whose collective fate was, for over sixty years, unaccounted for and undocumented.

Among the Republicans who fled Franco's Spain was Andrés Ordonez (1915-2001), the father of my friend Carlos who lives in Stroud. Andrés and some fellow refugees was given sanctuary at Whiteway and thus, Spanish anarchism and Republican utopianism were brought gently to rest close to Stroud and even closer to the estate where later, the Duke and Duchess of Kent lived at the end of the twentieth century century. *¡Olé!*

Other books and journals which have informed and influenced this piece include:

Joy Thacker, *Whiteway Colony: the social history of a Tolstoyan community* (self-published, Whiteway, 1993)

Anything by Colin Ward (many titles now published by Five Leaves and Freedom)

Chris Coates, *Utopia Britannica,* (Diggers and Dreamers, 2001)

Arthur Ransome, *Swallows and Amazons*

Robert Louis Stevenson, *Treasure Island* and *Travels with a Donkey*

George Orwell, *Homage to Catalonia*

Diane Di Prima, *Revolutionary Letters,* (Last Gasp, San Francisco)

Freedom: a hundred years 1886–1986, (Freedom Press)

Peace News

New Zealand and Utopianism in the 19th Century

John Lucas

I

Number 731 of Marianne North's water-colours housed at Kew Gardens is entitled "Entrance to the Otira Gorge, New Zealand". Painted on North's second world tour in 1881 (the first had been undertaken a decade earlier), during which she seems to have painted numerous scenes of all the places she visited, it shows a small settlement nestling at the base of a steep mountain range, remote, serene, and, so we might conclude, inaccessible. The view we have of settlement and gorge is framed between tall gum trees, so that North's vantage point inevitably suggests a squeezed-up landscape by Claude Lorraine, though the viewer looking through and beyond the trees is denied the suggestion of infinite recession common to Claude's paintings and achieved by the device of having a river wind its lazy way into the blue yonder, because here the mountain range acts as a drop curtain to block the view. As a result, the settlement seems at once safe and cut off.

The New Zealand poet Peter Bland describes the Otira Gorge, which is on the west coast half-way down the South Island, as providing a route through "the Southern Alps from the West Coast... to the inland places heading to Christchurch." The gorge, Bland writes, "is very dramatic with deep sides and a raging river," and it is, he adds, the subject of a famous painting by Petrus Van der Velden (1834–1913), which "has a big influence on later NZ landscape painters." From this I assume that North wasn't so much stumbling on a previously unknown scene as attracted to one already well-known and celebrated.

But celebrated as what? Look again at her painting. It isn't Claude, it isn't Richard Wilson, but in its modest way it is undoubtedly in the picturesque tradition. Years ago, I noted that this tradition took for granted that such landscape painting — and by extension, gardening and architecture — was not concerned with "moral, metaphysical, social or political matters."[1] Today, I would want to amend this to say that the picturesque *is* concerned with such matters but only in so far as they provide a view of the world from which history, in particular conflict, has been erased. The picturesque is essentially about what Duke Senior in *As You Like It* calls "the golden world." Prelapsarian. Paradisal. Innocent. Claude famously provided a melancholy tinge to his wonderful paintings by introducing into landscape crucial details that made plain the antiquity of the scene: classical ruins, classical deities, classical myths. This *was once* the world.

But no longer. *Et in Arcadia Ego*. Death dwells in Arcady. Like the lame boy in "The Pied Piper of Hamelin", we, the viewers, are forced to view a Claudian landscape as a scene from which we feel ourselves to be remote, because we live in a fallen world. The picturesque aesthetic is habituated to melancholy, even nostalgia, a word which came into existence in the 18th century. (It was created in order to identify the mental condition of Swiss Guards separated from their homeland, and is a compound of two Greek words: *nostos* = home and *algos* = pain.) In Wordsworth's "Immortality: An Ode", the adult poet looking back to his childhood is aware of an unbridgeable separation between then and now, and much 19th century literature, in England especially, attests to the psychological awareness, and costs, of living in a post-lapsarian world. Hardly surprising, given that the Industrial Revolution, begun in the 18th century, was increasingly understood to be accompanied by the obliteration of the past. Villages became towns, towns became cities, fields became factories, hitherto clean rivers became hopelessly polluted, social relations changed, the world of nature became increasingly remote, even for those who lived in rural circumstances. Hence John Clare's bitter grief at the enclosing of once common land:

"On paths to freedom and to childhood dear / A board sticks up to notice 'no road here.'"

Now look again at North's painting. In particular consider its title, "Entrance to the Otira Gorge, New Zealand". Leave aside questions of painterly skills. What makes her water-colour non-picturesque is the fact that we can imagine gaining entry not merely to a point of view but to the place itself. It isn't in the past. We don't look down from a high prospect onto a land receding into the unreachable distance. Nor are the buildings classical temples. They are contemporary, four-square domestic houses and, no doubt, outhouses. And within easy reach.

If this is Arcady, it is here and now. It is not only achievable, it has been achieved. People actually live here. Though there are in fact no people in North's picture, it is evident that the houses are in good condition and that the ground around them is tended. And the modest spires that can be seen on two of the structures suggest church and school. This is, you might say, not so much a vision of a lost utopia but its realisation in the present. This is a functioning community.

II

By the time North arrived at the Otira Gorge at least two English writers who had spent time in New Zealand had drawn on their experiences in order to imagine a form of contemporary utopianism. Such beginnings – such hopes – were of course common. From Coleridge and Southey's fleeting vision of establishing an ideal community of twelve couples on the banks of the Susquehanna (it was to be called Pantisocracy and its only achievement was the marriage of Coleridge and poor Sarah Fricker, who lived unhappily ever after), the 19th century was famously rich in belief that such dreams could be made flesh and blood. And if old, corrupt Europe wouldn't serve to nurture these communities, then the new world would. Go west, young man. Or south.

But not to Australia. White Australia was corrupted by being a convict settlement. No such taint attached itself to New Zealand. (I can't have been the only child who, coming across the name for the first time, thought it somehow suggested a new energy, new springiness of resolve.) With its mountains, rivers, forests and temperate climate, New Zealand was somehow like Britain, or anyway those parts of Europe with which the Brits were familiar and most comfortable. But it was Britain without the corruptions of modernity. In the 1830s, the historian Macaulay imagined the day when a New Zealander would stand on London Bridge, gazing on the ruins of a once mighty city. And Gustave Doré concluded his picture book of *London: a Pilgrimage* with the image of just such a New Zealander staring, lost in wonder, at "a stagnant Thames with a backdrop of mouldering wharves and warehouses and the distant, shattered dome of St Paul's."[2] New Zealand would provide a corrective vision to Britain's failures.

Doré's picture book was published in 1872, by necessary coincidence the year in which Samuel Butler's *Erewhon* first appeared. As Butler is nowadays something of a forgotten figure, it may help to sketch in his life up to the appearance of his first major publication. He was born in Langar, Nottinghamshire, where his father was vicar. An overbearing man, Butler senior, son of a Bishop, decided his own son should follow him into the church. Butler decided otherwise, and after Cambridge, from which he graduated in 1858, and the publication in 1859 of Darwin's *Origin of Species*, he refused point blank to do his father's bidding.[3] Nor was he willing to take to Law or Schoolmastering, on which Canon Butler fell back when it became clear that as far as his son was concerned the church was out. Instead, Butler proposed emigration. And having managed to winkle money of out Canon Butler, he went off to Canterbury, New Zealand, to earn his living as a sheep farmer. For a few years he did well at this and when, in 1864, he decided to sell up and return to England, he had enough money in his pocket to be able to lead an independent life. His plan was to succeed as an artist – he had genuine painterly skills – but it was *Erewhon* which made his name.

As commentators have noted, Butler's Nowhere is "Victorian England back to front", although as a society cut off from contact with the outside world Erewhon is self-sufficient, makes its own laws and customs – inversions for the most part of those Butler inbibed as a child – and, as G.D.H. Cole remarks in his short monograph, "machinery, instead of being worshipped as the source from which all blessings flow, [is] execrated and forbidden."[4] The place isn't flawless but it is certainly a corrective vision to what Butler thought of as the real horrors of the England in which he grew up: industrialisation and organised religion.

Erewhon carries as sub-title, *Over the Range*, and the setting is very obviously New Zealand. It is here the narrator comes at the start of the novel, as a young man seeking his fortune and delighted "with the country and the manner of life." But to get into Erewhon itself he must follow a river through a mountain range. Once beyond this, he finds himself in a land where, gazing into the distance, he can see "many a town and city, with buildings that had lofty steeples and rounded domes. Nearer beneath me lay ridge behind ridge, outline behind outline, sunlight behind shadow, and shadow behind sunlight, gully and serrated ravine. I saw large pine forests, and the glitter of a noble river winding its way upon the plains; also many villages and hamlets. Some of them quite near at hand..." (*Erewhon*: Penguin, 1954 edn. p.42) Steeples, domes, river, forests.... This is an amalgam of a Claudian landscape. More importantly for the present discussion, Erewhon is the great good place that lies open to the traveller who dares to overcome all difficulties set in his way, for which an apparently insuperable mountain range is as good a metaphor as any.

I have no idea whether North had read Butler's work – probably not – but looking at "Entrance to the Otira Gorge" with *Erewhon* in mind, we are likely to think that the settlement she shows us might well be home to adventurers who have succeeded in creating a new society, for themselves at least. It is necessary to cultivate your own garden, Voltaire insisted at the end of *Candide*, meaning that you should abandon grand dreams and seek contentment in your own life. But for both Butler and North, grand dream and modest cultivation of one spot come together. New Zealand is the vision of the great, good place made flesh, or anyway, earth.

Getting on for a quarter of a century earlier, in 1848, A.H. Clough published one of the best if least known of 19th century poems, "The Bothie of Ober-Na-Vuolich." The "Bothie" is a long, narrative poem — in the standard edition it runs to 58 pages — about a group of Oxford undergraduates who undertake a reading holiday in Scotland, accompanied by their tutor, "the grave man, nicknamed Adam ... Skilled in Ethics and Logic, in Pindar and Poets unrivalled;/*Shady* in Latin, said Lindsay, but *topping* in Plays and Aldrich." Lindsay, "the ready of speech, the Piper, the Dialectician," is one of the louche young men who make up the party, and there are others, who, with one exception, a young man called Philip Hewson, needn't detain us. It's enough to know that while they are on their reading jaunt they argue about issues of the day, including religion and politics, and, being young, they also talk of love. The talk is about ideal love, but then Philip falls in love with Elspie, the daughter of the crofter, in whose bothie they are staying. (A bothie or, as the OED gives it, "bothy" is a hut or cottage, often no more than one room, intended for rural labourers.) And this is where the poem becomes a great radical performance.

Performance is just. As with Clough's even greater *Amours de Voyage*, "The Bothie of Tober-Na-Vuolich" is written in hexameters, a form Clough handles with great skill and which he brilliantly moulds to the conversational, argumentative, disquisitional matter of his poem. It was Clough who complained about what he felt were the inadequacies of much contemporary poetry. By contrast, he said, novelists "do give us a real house to live in." In other words, novelists deal in day-today, substantial, bricky reality.

The "Bothie" is one of those novels in verse at which Clough's contemporaries, Browning above all, became expert. But it was Clough who showed the way. And not merely in achieving this technical, formal breakthrough. There is another breakthrough. Towards the end of the poem the young men, their reading party at an end, return to Oxford, though Philip does so reluctantly.

Philip returned to his books, but returned to his Highlands after;
Got a first, 'tis said; a winsome bride, 'tis certain.
There while courtship was ending, nor yet the wedding
appointed,
Under her father he studied the handling of hoe and
of hatcher ...
There did the four find Philip, the poet, the speaker,
the chartist,
Delving at Highland soil, and railing at Highland landlords ...

There is a certain keeping of distance here. Clough, or anyway the narrator, understands that Philip's democratic idealism can be a kind of posturing, Shelleyan in its ardency, and Shelleyan, perhaps, in its brevity, an Angel Clare *avant la lettre*, perhaps.

And yet at the end of the poem, Clough tells us that Philip and Elspie are married, and gone to New Zealand.

Five hundred pounds in pocket, with books, and two or three
pictures,
Tool-box, plough, and the rest, they rounded the sphere to
New Zealand.
There hew hewed and dug; subdued the earth and his spirit;
There he built him a home, there Elspie bore him his children,
David and Bella; perhaps ere this an Elspie and Adam;

There hath he farmstead and land, and fields of flax fields,
And the Antipodes too have a Bothie of Tober-na-vuolich.

"Farmstead and land". Why, it could be the settlement at Otira Gorge.

In his seminal essay, "1848 and the Strange Disease of Modern Love", John Goode tells us that Philip is in some respects based on Tom Arnold, brother of Clough's great friend, the more famous Matthew. Tom Arnold was a utopian socialist who set off, like Coriolanus, to find a world elsewhere. He thought he had found it in New Zealand, from where he wrote what are called his "Equator Letters" (1847), though the title under which they are published is *The New Zealand Letters of Thomas Arnold the Younger*, and in them he outlines his vision of an ideal democratic society. Goode is reasonably certain that Clough's Philip Hewson is at least partly modelled on Tom Arnold, and, as he notes, "The Bothie" "is not a poem about revolution, but a revolutionary poem about love... Precisely because it is such an affirmative poem about love, and love cannot merely be seen as a relief from or escape from the social structure, it necessarily becomes a radical critique of society and a vision of the possibilities of historical change."[5]

Philip and Elspie's marriage aligns two different classes, but its success seems to require them to abandon their homeland for a new world. There, they can work and bring up children and create a new Bothie: itself an image of work and culture reconciled rather than separated. (Toil for the working class, culture for the man of leisure.) "I am one of [the] rich class," Tom Arnold had written. "I have servants to wait upon me; I am fed and clothed by the labour of the poor, and do nothing for them in return. The life I lead is an outrage and a wrong to humanity." "The Bothie of Tober-na-Vuolich" provides a vision of how to counter that wrong. I am tempted to think that Clough self-consciously chose his male protagonist's name in order to bring together leisure/culture and work/toil. Philip (Astrophel — Sir Philip Sidney) and Hewson (son of a hewer, whether of wood or coal.) The earthly paradise is neither to be achieved nor sustained as that condition of "radiant idleness" which Orwell — wrongly — thought Dickens was after.

III

But paradise for one can be hell for another. The dream of making a Utopian society in New Zealand may be all very well. But did anyone ask the Maoris? What Arnold, Clough and Butler all leave out of account is the actual, troubled and sometimes bloody history of the European settlement of New Zealand as it developed throughout the nineteenth century. This isn't the place to set that out in any detail, but a few dates, some names and several facts, inevitably throw a murky light over the Claudian vision of a golden time restored. In 1840, shortly after Tom Arnold arrived in New Zealand, there were about two thousand whites living there. Twenty years later, when Samuel Butler landed, the number had risen to nearly 100,000, which still meant that Maoris outnumbered settlers by probably as many as twenty to one. Earlier in the century, white settlements had been few and far between, though missionaries were at work from 1814, at which time muskets were also introduced, tribal wars decimated native Maoris, and by 1839 "it could be claimed that peace and Christianity were in the ascendant". Well, that's nice to know. The following year, a Captain Hudson RN annexed the country to Australia "by peaceful arrangement with the natives". If they accepted the sovereignty of the queen, the Maoris were assured, they could keep possession of their lands, forests, and fisheries. But this reckoned without settlers who claimed they had bought the land from the natives. There were, inevitably therefore, further landings, squabbles, fights, and, in the words of one historian, then came "years of ruinous delay and official enquiry, during which Hudson died after founding Auckland. His successor, Fitzroy, drifted into an unsuccessful native war.... In 1852 the mother-country granted self-government... and a full parliamentary system and a responsible ministry was set going in 1856. For twenty years thereafter the political history of the colony consisted of two long, intermittent struggles," one constitutional, the other "racial — the conflict between the settler and the Maori. The native tribes, brave, intelligent and fairly well armed, tried, by means of a league against land-selling and the election of a king, to retain their hold at least over the central North Island." But they were eventually out-gunned, out-manoeuvered, and dispossessed. No paradise for them.

Notes

[1] "Wordsworth and the Anti-Picturesque" in my *Romantic to Modern Literature*, Harvester Press, 1982

[2] See William Feaver's introduction to *Boswell's London: Drawings by James Boswell*, Wildwood, 1978

[3] For his side of the argument and his unfavourable view of Canon Butler, see *The Way of All Flesh*

[4] *Samuel Butler and The Way of All Flesh*, G.D.H. Cole, Home & Van Thal, 1947, p.80

[5] In *Literature and Politics in the Nineteenth Century*, ed. John Lucas, Methuen 1971 & 1974, pp.45-76

Observations – New Lanark

Paul Barker

New Lanark is a bony place. The upper Clyde valley is soft and pretty, with green hills and tumbling water. Robert Owen's utopian company village is dropped in among this, like a sheep's weather-bleached skull.

Cotton manufacture, however high-principled, will never produce the architecture of fun. New Lanark is trumpeted now as a focus for tourism. Half a million people come here every year. It is a World Heritage Site. Owen's Institute for the Formation of Character is a visitor centre, selling tickets and brochures. But not even the discount shops (selling cardigans at £2.95) or the recreation of the Owenite store (plastic bacon, priced at 8p a pound) can disguise the underlying sternness of it all.

And jollity comes with a message. In the café at No. 3 Mill, you can put your head through holes in cut-out pictures, and be photographed as a cloth-capped workman or a pinafored woman. You can buy "a children's toy from a bygone era": a "gird and cleek" (a child's hoop and iron, to the English), forged in Scotland.

It is a reinvention of Scottish tradition. I am reminded of Hugh Trevor-Roper's celebrated demolition job on the myth of tartan. You can have a full selection of stickers: "It's hard to be humble when you are Scottish", "Honk if you are Scottish" and "Anything can happen in a kilt". The New Lanark kilt shop has a special offer of the complete works (own choice of tartan) for £439: Argyll jacket, Montrose belt, kilt and kilt pin, hose and flashes, ghillie brogues, "semi-dress sporran".

Owen echoed the Hollywood studio joke: "The son-in-law also rises." New Lanark was built up by his father-in-law, a self-made Glasgow banker. In a classic career move, Owen married the boss's daughter. He helped himself to become a socialist hero by losing all his money at his disastrous follow-up utopia of New Harmony in Indiana.

New Lanark had risen to prosperity on the back of child labour and poverty-stricken migrants from the Highlands and Ireland. Most of the Irish were Ulster Presbyterians, so New Lanark escaped the sectarian battles which are far from dead in the politics of the west of Scotland. Owen wanted to create a world without religious or class divisions. But there is something chilling, in 1998, about his gospel, *A New View of Society*: "I hesitate not to say, that the members of any community may by degrees be trained to live *without idleness, without poverty, without crime, and without punishment*."

Or again: "The kind or degree of misery or happiness experienced by the members of any community, depend on the characters which have been formed in the individuals which constitute the community. It becomes, then, of the highest interest, and consequently the first and most important duty, of every state, to form the individual characters of which the state is composed."

The Rochdale Pioneers started their co-ops on "Owenite principles." But nobody was obliged to shop at a co-op. Owen's shop at New Lanark was a company store. Workpeople got tokens instead of cash. Better food, perhaps, at lower prices; but also a way of controlling what workers bought, especially drink.

New Lanark tottered on till 1968. It has been exquisitely restored. Scottish Nuclear chipped in, by refitting a black-and-red engine, gleaming with bright brass pipes and knobs. (Back to the future?) But walking around between the mills and the model tenements, I feel surrounded by the symbolism of the early welfare state. The bell-turret reminds me of workhouses, the Institute reminds me of orphanages, the mills could just as easily be Poor Law infirmaries.

Go to any NHS hospital, and you soon see the latter-day welfare state has not shaken off that taint, that we should somehow all be *grateful*.

I assume that Alistair Gray named the hero of his great novel *Lanark* with Owen's utopias in mind. Gray saw, and mocked, the dismal postwar landscape of autocratic Scottish socialism, much of which claimed to derive from Owen. You could parody it as old men, in chains of office, snipping the ribbons to declare open 31-storey tower blocks or motorways from nowhere to nowhere.

The 1991 Penguin collection of Owen's writings observes: "Gerontocracy has become the mode of rule in many nominally socialist countries, for many of the same reasons Owen thought it appropriate." (He saw age-power, with rule by elders, as the most rational form of government.) Writing just before the Soviet Union collapsed, the Penguin editor added: "far too few communist leaders have proved to be as benevolent as Mr Owen."

You could say that again. And you could say the same of the long rule of Scotland's Labour gerontocracy.

On the cover of his next book after *Lanark*, Gray embossed this motto: "Work as if you were living in the early days of a better nation." Much of New Lanark was restored by young people on various cheap-labour anti-unemployment schemes. The new hotel, inserted into the rebuilt No. 1 Mill, says: "Opened for business 1785, opened for pleasure 1998."

In Search of Utopia Down the Pub

Ross Bradshaw

Mike Pentelow and Peter Arkell know more about the inside and outside of pubs than most people, having written *A Pub Crawl through History* (Janus, 2010). Being socialists, it is hardly a surprise that they found many pubs that mark socialist or rebellious events or celebrate well-known socialists or rebels in addition to the usual fare of highwaymen and inventors. These include The Robin Hood Inn (Edwinstowe), The Hero of Switzerland i.e. William Tell (Camberwell), The Wat Tyler, commemorating the leader of the Peasants' Revolt of 1381 (Dartford), Owain Glyndwr (Cardiff and Beaumaris)... and we are only up to page 13. Apart from Tyler, other rural champions include Robert Kett, commemorated in Wymondham and Norwich and the poet John Clare at Gunthorpe, near Peterborough. The rural rebellion with the most lasting significance was at Tolpuddle, home of what is now an annual trade union festival, and the home of the Martyrs Inn, commemorating those members of the Tolpuddle Friendly Society of Agricultural Labourers who were transported to Australia and where the Methodist George Loveless wrote the Song of Freedom:

God is our guide, from field, from wave,
From plough, from anvil and from loom;
We come, our country's right to save.
And speak a tyrant faction's doom;
We raise the watchword liberty,
We will, we will, we will be free!

And so they were, after an enormous campaign by the fledgling labour movement, as depicted in a mural on the side of a former pub, the former Mitre in Copenhagen Street, North London. Also transported, this time for more direct action, was Elizabeth Parker, who took part in the Captain Swing agricultural riots. She was captured at what became The Trouble House Inn in Tetbury, where she was arrested along with twenty-two of her fellow machine wreckers. There is also the Joseph Arch inn, at Barford, another marker of the struggle for better conditions for agricultural workers.

Photo © Peter Arkell

Other types of campaigners recognised include Richard Oastler, in Brighouse, campaigner against child labour who also campaigned against slavery, as did William Wilberforce (Kingston-upon-Hull and, sadly now a private house, East Farleigh). Ireland of course has many pubs celebrating Republicans, though the Charlotte Despard is on the Archway Road in London, while St Albans boasts The Garibaldi. More surprising is The Independent on the Caledonian Road in London, which remembers the fighter for Hungarian Independence, Lajos Kossuth.

More directly on the utopian front, The Land of Liberty, Peace and Plenty in Heronsgate, in Hertfordshire, "takes its name from an adjoining Chartist settlement called O'Connorville after its founder Feargus O'Connor. This was a land experiment, organised by O'Connor, to provide smallholdings to working men as an alternative to factory employment. Shares were advertised in the *Northern Star* in 1845 and those who bought them for a few pennies a week qualified for a lottery for plots of land. Enough money flooded in to purchase five settlements around the country, the first of which was 105 acres at Heronsgate, which was to be divided into thirty-five plots, each with a cottage; previously the entire farm was cultivated by three men and a boy. ... A school was also built and crops sown in time for the grand opening on May Day 1847, when the settlers took over their land." The colony beer shop became the Land of Liberty in honour of the Chartist settlement, in 1870, though the colony itself had already been wound up. Another Chartist pictured on a pub sign is William Lovett, at The Chartist in Skelmanthorpe. Lovett was a co-operator as well as a trade unionist and he drew up the actual People's Charter. Five of the six Chartist demands were eventually won.

Of the modern pubs connected to trade unions, the Flying Picket in Liverpool is, alas, but a memory, though the trade union owned Bread and Roses pub in Battersea thrives in conjunction with the Workers' Beer Company, often to be seen pulling pints at festivals. There is no modern equivalent, perhaps, of Samuel Plimsoll, remembered by The Plimsoll Line in his home town of Redcar. Plimsoll stopped the sailing of "coffin-ships", described in *A Pub Crawl through History* as being "unseaworthy, overloaded and heavily overinsured vessels, the owners of which were happy to see them sink in order to collect the inflated, and often fraudulent compensation". Owners resisted the "line" in question, a load-line to prevent overcrowding. One MP, Edward Bates, had lost three ships with a total loss of eighty-seven lives in one year. Plimsoll described such men as "maritime murderers."

William Morris will need no introduction. Though no teetotaller he despised "the drink-steeped liquor shops". Morris has two pubs named after him, one in Hammersmith, the other, at Merton Abbey Mill, "was originally Liberty's block shop, where their printing blocks of Morris's designs were stowed, some of which are framed on the walls." John Jacques does, however, need an introduction. A miner at thirteen, he became one of this country's leading co-operators and chief executive of the Portsea Island Mutual Cooperative Society and author of that essential volume *Management Accounting*. The public house named after him stands where one of his old co-ops used to be. There are many other key figures: Oscar Wilde, whose name now graces a pub in Berlin, Rupert Brooke, who described himself as "a William Morris sort of socialist", has a pub in his name in Grantchester. Given the nature of this volume I've excluded the cricketers, the authors, singers and body-snatchers, but the book is endlessly interesting even though some of the pubs mentioned are bound to have closed or changed hands since publication.

Mike Pentelow and Peter Arkell end their book with a little utopian dreaming of their own, reporting on the campaign to have The Running Mare at Cobham renamed after Gerrard Winstanley and the Diggers who worked and ate bread together on the nearby St George's Hill. Tony Benn and Billy Bragg have backed the campaign. The suggest further name changes which would give Peter Kropotkin supporters a place to down the odd shandy but more realistically to rename the Burston Crown in honour of Kitty and Tom Higdon whose twenty-five year school strike is still celebrated on the first Sunday of September. But best of all would be if the Baraka Cocktail Bar in Hastings could be renamed in honour of Robert Tressell for that is "where workers would try to get jobs by buying foremen drinks" or the

John's Cross Inn where "the works beano... was recorded so splendidly in the *Ragged Trousered Philanthropists"*. I'll drink to that.

Contributors

From 1996 to 1999, **Paul Barker** wrote a weekly *New Statesman* column about places, under the title Observations. The New Lanark column appeared in August 1988. Long-time editor of *New Society*, launched fifty years ago on 2 October 1962, and now a senior research fellow at the Young Foundation, Paul Barker's recent books include *Arts in Society* (revised edition, Five Leaves, 2006), *The Freedoms of Suburbia* (Frances Lincoln, 2009) and *Hebden Bridge: a sense of belonging* (Frances Lincoln, 2012). His Observation column on Leeds was reprinted in *Maps*.

Marie Louise Berneri died in 1949, at the age of thirty-one. The essay here is taken from her *Journey Through Utopia*, which was published after her death and is reprinted by permission of Freedom Press. Marie Louise Berneri was a lifelong anarchist. Her books included *Neither East Nor West* and *Workers in Stalin's Russia*. She was on the editorial groups of the journals *Revolt*, *War Commentary* and *Freedom*.

Ross Bradshaw has been the publisher at Five Leaves since 1995.

Ian Clayton is a broadcaster, documentary maker, storyteller and author. His *Bringing It All Back Home* was a small press best-seller for Route, a book that wandered from Featherstone to the Mississippi, making a connection. He is also the author of *Our Billie*, written after the accidental death of his daughter. Read more at www.ianclayton.info.

Jeff Cloves lives in the People's Republic of Stroud. A poet, cyclist and footballer, he writes a regular column for

Peace News. In 2011 he jointly organised a festival celebrating the Spanish poet Federico García Lorca. He has been a member of Riffraffpoets since 1970.

Will Buckingham writes fiction, philosophy and for children. When not writing, he is a senior lecturer in Creative Writing in the School of Humanities at De Montfort University. His most recent books include the children's book, *The Snorgh and the Sailor*, a novel, *The Descent of the Lyre*, and a philosophy book on happiness, *Introducing Happiness*. Find out more at www.willbuckingham.com. He is also one of the organisers of the States of Independence project.

Gilian Darley has written biographies of Sir John Soane and Octavia Hill, the latter recently re-issued in a new edition. Her book *Vesuvius* was a Radio 4 Book of the Week. Her 1975 book, *Villages of Vision — a study of strange utopias* was published in a new edition by Five Leaves in 2007. Together with David McKie, she is writing a collection of essays on Ian Nairn, *Nairnscape*, to be published by Five Leaves in late 2013. Her essay 'Ian Nairn: taking Jack Kerouac on the road' appeared in *Maps*.

Dennis Hardy's latest book is *From Garden Cities to New Towns; campaigning for town and country planning 1899-1946*. His previous books include *Alternative Communities in Nineteenth Century England* and, with Colin Ward, *Arcadia for All*. His current research is about liveable cities.

Pippa Hennessy works at Five Leaves Publications. She is also secretary of Nottingham Poetry Society and one of the organisers of Nottingham Festival of Words. She blogs at http://battypip.wordpress.com.

John Lucas runs Shoestring Press in Nottingham. He is a poet, a critic, a writer on cricket and a jazz musician. His latest book is a novel, *Waterdrops*, published by Greenwich Exchange. His essay 'Uprisings in the South West' appeared in *Maps*. Among his publications for Five Leaves are the poetry collection *Things to Say* and *Next Year Will Be Better: a memoir of England in the 1950s*.

Haywire Mac (Harry Kirkby McLintock) was a member of the IWW and an American singer who claimed to have written The Big Rock Candy Mountains, later popularised by Burl Ives.

Mike Marqusee is a journalist. He has published books on Bob Dylan, Muhammed Ali and cricket. His most recent books include the memoir *If I Am Not for Myself: Journey of an Anti-Zionist Jew* and *Street Music*, a collection of poetry. A version of the essay included here first appeared in *Red Pepper*. See www.mikemarqusee.com.

William Morris's essay 'A Factory As It Might Be' appeared in 1884. It was first paired with Colin Ward's essay in this collection in a 1994 pamphlet published by Mushroom Bookshop.

Chris Moss has been the books and travel editor of *Time Out*. You can find more of his travel journalism at www.chris-moss.net. He is the author of *Patagonia: a cultural history*.

Deirdre O'Byrne teaches Irish and English literature at Loughborough University and in various community settings. She is a member of Nottingham Irish Studies Group. Her essay 'The Way to the Past': Eavan Boland's remapping of Irish history, appeared in *Maps*.

Ian Parks first appeared in the famous Hull anthology, *Rumoured City* in 1982. Since then he has published many collections, his latest being *The Exile's House*

(Waterloo Press). His poem 'The Land of Green Ginger' appeared in *Maps*. He is the editor of the anthology *A Version of the North: Contemporary Yorkshire Poetry*, to be published by Five Leaves in 2013.

John Payne has written a city guide to Bath and a cultural history of the West Country, both for Signal. His books for Five Leaves include a cultural history of Catalonia and *Journey up the Thames: William Morris and Modern England*. His essay on Walter Benjamin, 'Death on the Border' appeared in *Maps*.

Peter Preston, to whom this volume is dedicated, was an adult education lecturer, the founder of the D.H. Lawrence Research Centre at the University of Nottingham, and former editor of the journal of the William Morris Society. He was a popular speaker at academic conferences and local book festivals and a great supporter of the independent publishing sector, including Five Leaves. Peter died in 2011. His essay printed here first appeared in a longer version published by the William Morris Society, being the Annual Kelmscott Lecture given at the Art Workers' Guild in 2002. The essay is published by permission of the William Morris Society and Barbara Preston.

Andrew Rigby's books on communes, both published in 1974, *Alternative Realities* and *Communes in Britain*, are still core reading for anyone researching intentional communities. His book *Living the Intifada* (now available free, online at http://civilresistance.info/rigby1991) was the first book to examine the Intifada, including discussion of violence and nonviolence. He has long been associated with the journal *Peace News*, and peace education in general.

David Rosenberg leads guided walks round the East End of London. He is an active member of the National Union of Teachers and has been a member of the editorial board of *Jewish Socialist* magazine since it began in the

1980s. He is the author of *Battle for the East End: Jewish responses to fascism in the 1930s* (Five Leaves).

Leon Rosselson is a singer/songwriter and a children's author. Last year he celebrated fifty years of performing and his 75th birthday. The boxed set *The World Turned Upside Down* comprises 72 songs from across his career, over four CDs, available from www.leonrosselson.co.uk.

J. David Simons is a full time writer, living in Glasgow. His novels, *The Credit Draper* and *The Liberation of Celia Kahn,* are set in the Jewish community in Glasgow around the first world war. He is currently working on *The Land Agent*, which is partly set in a young kibbutz in the Jordan Valley in the 1920s, which will be published by Five Leaves in 2014. See www.jdavidsimons.com.

Paul Summers was founding co-editor of the magazines *Billy Liar* and *Liar Republic*. He currently lives in Australia. His latest collection is *union* published by Smokestack, which includes 'the shadow of chimneys', published here. He was one of three poets, the others being Andy Croft and W.N. Herbert, published as *Three Men on the Metro* by Five Leaves.

Mandy Vere has been at News from Nowhere Bookshop (www.newsfromnowhere.org.uk) in Liverpool since 1976 and imagines she will eventually be carried out. A version of her essay on News from Nowhere first appeared in *North West Labour History*.

Colin Ward was the chronicler of the unofficial landscape. His books covered squatting, allotments, the water crisis, the plotlands of the South East, transport and anarchism. He was the editor of *Anarchy* magazine and *BEE* — the bulletin of environmental education. Five Leaves published the collection *Remembering Colin Ward 1924-2010* after his death.

Ken Worpole has written on Essex before, in *350 Miles: an Essex Journey*. His other books include those on the hospice movement, town planning and graveyard art. His book on working class writers of an earlier era, *Dockers and Detectives* was first published by Verso and issued in a revised edition by Five Leaves. He contributed an introduction to *King Dido* by Alexander Baron (New London Editions). See www.worpole.net.

Selected Five Leaves Books by Contributors to *Utopia*

Arts in Society
Edited by Paul Barker
Essays by Angela Carter, John Berger, Reyner Banham, Michael Wood, Dennis Potter and others
316 pages, 978 1 905512 07 2, £9.99

Villages of Vision: a study of strange utopias
Gillian Darley
339 pages, illustrated, 978 0 907123 50 7, £14.99

Next Year Will Be Better: a memoir of England in the 1950s
John Lucas
416 pages, 978 1 907869 29 7, £9.99

Things to Say
Poetry by John Lucas
76 pages, 978 1 905512 92 8, £7.99

Catalonia: history and culture
John Payne
2nd edition, 339 pages, 978 1 905512 82 9, £10.99

Journey up the Thames: William Morris and Modern England
John Payne
224 pages, 978 0 90712368 2, £7.99

Battle for the East End: Jewish responses to fascism in the 1930s
David Rosenberg
268 pages, 978 1 907869 18 1, £9.99

The Credit Draper
A novel by J. David Simons
350 pages, 978 1 907869 02 0, £8.99

The Liberation of Celia Kahn
A novel by J. David Simons
272 pages, 978 1 907869 03 7, £8.99

Three Men on the Metro
Poems by Andy Croft, W.N. Herbert and Paul Summers
121 pages, 978 1 905512 84 3, £7.99

Talking Green
Twelve essays by Colin Ward
136 pages, 978 1 907869 51 8, £7.99

Cotters and Squatters
Colin Ward
176 pages, 978 0 907123 19 4, £9.99

Dockers and Detectives
Ken Worpole
160 pages, 978 1 905512 37 9, £8.99

Available from bookshops or, post free, from
www.fiveleaves.co.uk

Maps

A quirky compendium of essays on maps, places and people, many by leading writers, including Iain Sinclair and *The Guardian*'s David McKie and Chris Arnot, as well as writers from the *London Review of Books*, academic journals, a journalist from the BBC World Service and several biographers.

Iain Sinclair	Walking Through Liverpool
Chris Arnot	Lost Cricket Grounds of England
David Belbin	Graham Greene in Nottingham
Ross Bradshaw & Ian Parks	The Land of Green Ginger
Andy Croft	Reading Poetry in Siberia
Richard Dennis	Mapping Gissing's Novels
Gillian Darley	Ian Nairn and Jack Kerouac: On the Road
Roberta Dewa	Wilford: An English Village in the 1950s
John Lucas	Uprisings in the South West
David McKie	The Mapping of Surnames
Deirdre O'Byrne	The Famine Roads of Ireland
John Payne	Death on the Border: Walter Benjamin
Mark Patterson	A Short Walk up Dere Street
Andrew Whitehead	Beyond Boundary Passage: London Fiction
Sara Jane Palmer	A Walk to Tafraoute
Paul Barker	The Other Britain: Leeds
Robert Macfarlane	The Guga Men

"a curious rattle-bag of writing"
Guardian

"reading (*Maps*) is akin to peeling back layers, deciphering faded contours and occasionally, redrawing an entire geography. If travel journalism wants to adapt to the recession, here's a direction it might follow."
Time Out

2011, 159 pages, 978 1 907869 24 2, £7.99

Crime

Five Leaves, 2013 compendium will include Jon McGregor on coroners' courts, John Harvey on Z-Cars, Peter Mortimer on his days as a junior court reporter on a local newspaper, John Stuart Clark on working semi-illegally as a scrappy, Alan Dent on One Day in Whitehaven, Russel D McLean on his favourite crime writer, Danuta Reah on forensic linguistics, David Belbin on turning hometown crime into fiction, Rod Madocks on suicide... and many more essays on the loose theme of crime.

2013, c.200 pages, 978 1 907869 79 2, £9.99

Available from bookshops or, post free, from www.fiveleaves.co.uk

THE COUNTRY STANDARD

Vol. I No. 2 APRIL, 1936 Price 1d.